QUEEN ELIZABETH

by Charles Williams

the apocryphile press

BERKELEY, CA

www.apocryphile.org

apocryphile press
BERKELEY, CA

Apocryphile Press
1700 Shattuck Ave #81
Berkeley, CA 94709
www.apocryphile.org

First published by The Camelot Press, Ltd., 1936.
First Apocryphile edition, 2010.

For sale in the USA only. Sales prohibited in the UK.
Printed in the United States of America.

ISBN 978-1-933993-99-7

CONTENTS

CHRONOLOGY

1533....Birth of Elizabeth.

1537....Birth of Edward VI.

1547....Death of Henry VIII. Seymour marries Queen Catherine Parr.

1549....Arrest of Seymour; examination of Elizabeth.

1553....Accession of Mary.

1554....Elizabeth imprisoned in the Tower (18 March); removed to Woodstock (14 May); marriage of Mary.

1558....Death of Mary; Accession of Elizabeth.

1559....Coronation of the Queen. First-Parliament; the English service again used; reformation of the finances; beginning of the courtships.

1560....Treaty of Edinburgh; rise of Dudley; death of Amy Robsart.

1561....Return of Mary Stuart to Scotland; English troops in France; Francis Bacon born.

1562....Hawkins's first slave voyage.

1564....Robert Dudley made Earl of Leicester; Marlowe and Shakespeare born.

1565....Marriage of Mary Stuart and Darnley.

1567....Flight of Mary Stuart.

1569....Norfolk conspiracy and Northern Rebellion.

1570....The Pope issues Bull of Deposition :
Regnans in Excelsis.

1571....Beginning of the Anjou courtship ; first
official persecution.

1572....Ridolfi Plot ; execution of Norfolk ;
beginning of the Alençon (Anjou)
courtship.

1580....Coming of the Jesuit missionaries ;
Raleigh knighted ; Drake completes
voyage round the world.

1581....Edmund Campion executed.

1584....Death of Alençon ; assassination of
William of Orange ; the Instrument of
Association.

1586....The Babington Plot ; execution of Mary
Stuart.

1587....Essex becomes Master of the Horse ; Sir
C. Hatton Lord Chancellor.

1588....Spanish Armada ; death of the Earl of
Leicester.

1593....Death of Marlowe.

1598....Deaths of Philip of Spain and Burghley.

1599....Essex Lieutenant of Ireland.

1601....Execution of Essex ; reconciliation of the
Queen and Commons on Monopolies.

1603....Death of Elizabeth.

CHAPTER I

THE life of Elizabeth represents, in English history, the longest and most spectacular period of a change in society. That change began before her, and was not concluded until long after her. It was the change from a society directed, at any rate in theory, by a metaphysical idea, to a society directed, both in theory and practice, by nothing but the continual pressure of events. It is a change completed in our own day ; beyond our present political accommodation to events we cannot go. We are on the point of discovering whether that accommodation is sufficient, or whether we must return to a metaphysical idea – either that of the past or some other.

This change in society was unintended, through Europe at large as through England in particular. It took place because the results of all human action are always different from anything intended or expected. No ruler and no

statesman of the Elizabethan period – except
perhaps Maitland of Lethington – wished to
abolish metaphysical ideas from their place in
society. Elizabeth no more definitely desired it
than did Philip of Spain. Both she and he proposed that all events in their dominions should
be subordinated to themselves, and to the metaphysical schemes which they respectively held.
The nature of Philip held very intensely to his
metaphysical scheme ; the nature of Elizabeth
much more lightly to hers. She was vividly and
personally aware of events ; he, impersonally
and abstractly. In the great medieval society
of Europe which preceded them there had been
many rulers who resembled one or the other ;
some had tended to beliefs, some to events, but
their natures, in every case, had been modified
by the nature of the whole society. Before the
rise of Elizabeth and Philip that society had
received two violent shocks, both of which compelled princes to take immediate cognizance of
beliefs other than their own. A belief other than
one's own is not, to oneself, a belief ; it is an
event.

The metaphysics of medieval Europe consisted
of two correlated parts. The first part included
the nature of God and the soul ; the second,
the temporal nourishment and instruction of
the soul. The first dealt, largely, with the person and life of our Saviour ; the second with the

visible Church, the nature of the Sacraments, and the ordering of morals. The first has throughout the history of Christendom remained practically untouched, except by a few scattered and suppressed teachers ; it was the second part that received the shocks, first, of the Great Schism, and, second, of the Reformation.

The Great Schism of the West concerned the person – but not primarily the office – of the Pope. It began when, in 1378, during the pontificate of Urban VI, certain Cardinals, fleeing from Rome, elected one of their number to the Papacy under the name of Clement VII. In theory, the organization of the Church remained unaffected by this action ; one of the two, and later three, claimants was the true Pope, and the true Pope was the true Pope, however many claimants there might be. In fact, however, that organization suffered throughout Europe all kinds of controversies and compromises. Not only were the religious nerves of Europe seriously shaken, but a considerable impetus was given to a movement already in progress – the Rise of the Nations. This rise, which had many causes, had many results, one of the most important of which was what may be called a deflection of mass. Medieval Europe had theoretically considered the mass of mankind as one, which was the Church, corresponding to the One Man which was Christ. There were heretics and infidels, but they were an outrage on the unity of mankind. Theoretically, mankind and Christendom were identical ; anything else was disease. But however much the laws of belief still compelled attention to this supreme mass which was mankind, the laws of events during and after the Schism compelled a much more immediate attention to those smaller masses which were the nations. The shadowy headship of the Emperor, and the substantial headship of the Pope, lost something of their prestige. National, or at least dynastic, glory obtruded itself upon universal glory. The close of the Schism was followed by the continual rise of these secondary national glories, and by an accompanying weariness with metaphysics after the strain of the Schism, which in turn assisted, even in the case of the Popes themselves, the other glory of the Renascence.

This variation preceded the second metaphysical shock which Europe received ; namely, the outbreak of the Reformation. This second shock, again, was not directed against the primal idea of Christianity – of redemption through the Double Nature and supernatural interposition of Christ. But it very seriously affected all ideas of the nature of the visible Church, of the Sacraments, and of the official direction of morals. The question of the Papacy itself was only one among a number of questions, and was not everywhere regarded as of the first importance. The

Council of Trent had not yet met ; nor had the Roman Church, as it now is, been adequately formulated. On that and other subjects, however, a new series of other people's beliefs – that is, of events – came into violent existence. The sovereigns of Europe had to deal with these events, and had to deal with them not as sporadic but as continuous. Heresy (whatever, in a short time, that came to mean in each State) was no longer a person, a sect, or even an idea ; it had become an unbroken and militant series of persons, sects, and ideas. It was a permanent hostility outside each State and a permanent threat of revolt within, a threat acutely felt by the developed sense of royal and national glory which pervaded the kingdoms.

In England the serious dispute began not with metaphysics but with morals. The King of England, Henry VIII, had indeed written a book against Luther, a champion of the new metaphysics, and had been saluted as *Defender of the Faith* by the Pope. His marriage had been arranged by a special action on the part of the Pope. He had married his brother Arthur's widow, by dispensation from the Papal authority, representing a moral law which normally forbade men to marry their brothers' widows. It was pontifically declared that Catherine of Aragon had not been Arthur's wife, and that Henry might justly marry her. The King very

greatly desired a male heir. Unfortunately, in
the next sixteen years Catherine bore five children – four stillborn, another dying just after
birth. She had one child who lived, the daughter
Mary. Presently she was beyond childbearing.
It was clear that God had refused an heir to
Henry by Catherine. The state of Henry's mind
has received little sympathy, since nowadays
few of us desire children, fewer marry their
brothers' widows, and still fewer believe that
there is a moral law forbidding such marriages.
To understand his decision it is necessary to
understand his dilemma : was God displeased
at his marriage ? His emotions said *yes* ; the
old metaphysic said *no*. It was an age in which
natural events were held to be supernaturally
significant, and, had circumstances been reversed,
it is certain that Henry's five dead children would
have been declared by the vocal champions of
the Church to be very certain signs of God's
displeasure.

Another series of events intensified the King's
emotional crisis, and assisted its resolution : their
name was Anne Boleyn. Henry fell violently in
love with her ; she demanded marriage. The
King's fear, the King's hope, the King's desire,
combined to urge him to discover a solution of
his problem other than that maintained – but
only just maintained – at Rome. Negotiations
broke down. There was, of course, never any

divorce between him and Catherine, but a decree
of nullity was issued by English ecclesiastical
authority without Roman assent. The breach
between two metaphysics concerning the nature
of the visible Church was immediately present.
It was followed by an immediate and official
intensification of an attack on the wealth and
power of the clergy in England which had been
for some time officially in motion. The monasteries were dissolved.

The decree of nullity was pronounced by
Cranmer in May 1533. The King had been
privately married to Anne in December 1532.
The Princess Elizabeth was born in the following September. Three months afterwards she
was given her own royal household at Hatfield,
and her elder sister, the Lady Mary, now publicly
declared illegitimate, was commanded to form
part of the Court that circled round the unconscious interloper. In another sense also Elizabeth
was an interloper : the King had been hoping
for a male heir. But he was gracious, and proceeded to take steps further to define the situation. In 1534 an Act and Oath of Succession
was promulgated, by which the marriage with
Catherine was declared " against the laws of
God " and the marriage with Anne " perfect
ever." A mass of detail concerning marriage and
prohibited degrees was included in the Act and
therefore in the Oath, as also was a renunciation

of any contrary oath "to any other within
the realm, or foreign authority, prince, or poten-
tate." The Oath was almost universally received,
by laity and clergy alike. John Fisher, Bishop
of Rochester, refused ; so, in spite of the earnest
entreaty of the Abbot of Westminster, and others,
did Sir Thomas More. It may be allowed that
they kept their integrity, but it is impossible to
believe that all the rest of the hierarchy and the
priesthood deliberately and consciously abandoned their own. A much more severe Oath,
expressly repudiating the jurisdiction of the
Roman See " and its laws, decrees, and canons,
if any of them should be found contrary to the
law of God and Holy Scripture," was addressed
to all orders of friars and monks ; it was refused
only in three places. Meanwhile the fleet of the
King of France hovered in the seas ready to
assist against Catherine's cousin, the Emperor,
if he should desire to interfere. Convocation,
north and south, with five dissentients, resolved
that by Holy Scripture the Bishop of Rome had
no greater jurisdiction in England than any other
bishop ; the Universities assented. In February
1535 all the bishops explicitly renounced the
primacy of the See of Rome ; a number of them
wrote felicitating the King on his action. They
provided for similar acts on the part of all their
clergy. The same year saw the execution of
More, Fisher, a small number of recalcitrant

monks, and twice as many otherwise recalcitrant Anabaptists. Under such auspices the legitimacy of the child Elizabeth was declared and upheld ; to this extent the events of the dead children and of Anne had shaken the pattern of metaphysical theory.

Nevertheless, in the very next year her legitimacy was, in a few days, utterly and royally denied. The life of the Courts of the Renascence was as bloody and spectacular as its plays ; its palaces were full of a perilous domesticity, and what actual life could not attain common report provided. Fact, rumour, and imagination mingled their melodrama. The peculiarity of Henry was his passionate desire to be moral, and even legal, in his marriages and murders. In that certainly he was less than strong ; his spirit demanded popular support, and he took steps to ensure it. The weakness exposed him to something like blackmail ; the lands of the clergy formed an unspoken union between the Catholic lords and their Catholic sovereign. But that bargain was separate from, though politically related to, the theological controversy ; the unhappy figure of Cranmer unites them. He was concerned for the truth of doctrine, and he was involved in the falsehood of politics. He is a shy literary figure among those crimson Renascence splendours and terrors, and singularly out of place.

Be

In January 1536 Anne Boleyn gave birth to a prince ; the child, as if celestial anger renewed itself against the Throne, was born dead. Again the superstition and the lust of the King grew together, but this time, Anne being his own subject, and he being more used to action, he struck more violently. On 2 May, accused of great and heinous crimes, Anne was sent to the Tower ; on 17 May, in the vaults of Lambeth, the marriage was declared by Cranmer, on the evidence laid before him, to be *nullum, invalidum, et inane*. On 19 May the wretched woman was executed. In June the Parliament also declared the marriage void, and the Princess Elizabeth illegitimate. In the eyes of Rome and half Europe she was already so ; she was now to be so to all England. It became treason for anyone to assert the legitimacy either of her or of her half-sister Mary, though, by a fantastic logic worthy of the theatre itself, the penalties against all those who had previously declared her illegitimate still remained in force. Meanwhile, Catherine and Anne both being dead, Henry achieved his first indubitably valid marriage – with Jane Seymour. Could events be certainly related to ideas, the result might be held to have justified all his doubts, all his denials, and all his destructions – a male heir was conceived, and born in July of 1537. So swift a celestial justification of his action must have hardened through his future life the King's

belief in his own interpretation of doctrine and
morals. The Lady Mary and the Lady Elizabeth
were brought, from that joint household to which
now they were both reduced, Elizabeth as the
junior member, to be present at their legitimate
brother's baptism. His mother, Jane, ensured
the legal future of her son by dying soon after the
ceremony.

The King had some virtue ; he held no grudge
against the children of his disasters. By 1544 he
even established both his daughters in the right
of succession to the Throne. They remained
formally illegitimate, but the bar sinister was to
be merely ignored ; *le Roi le veult.* The small
Elizabeth grew ; she had difficulty with her
teeth ; they came slowly – " causeth me," wrote
her governess, Lady Bryan, " to suffer her Grace
to have her will more than I would." With
her mental teeth she had no difficulty – " a
toward child." In the same year, 1544, when she
was ten years old, she was translating French
devotional poetry. Tutors were appointed –
from the group of Cambridge humanists who
represented more particularly the New Learning, and therefore the Reforming party. The
intellectual influences brought to bear on her
through the years of her education were those
of " true religion " as distinguished from the
" old Faith." To scholarship she grew easily –
Greek and Latin ; and modern languages –

French and Italian and Spanish. " Her mind,"
wrote Ascham, " has no womanly weakness."
Elizabeth would not have thanked him for the
adjective. Whatever she admired in her mas-
culine Court of later years was not the mental
capacity of its members ; nor did she need.

In 1547 Henry died. Edward VI, at ten years
old, began to reign, and his uncle, Edward
Seymour, became Earl of Somerset and Protector of the Kingdom. The blackmail of the
old reign ceased, and a simpler process of direct
seizure was substituted. The Lady Elizabeth,
then thirteen, was moved to the guardianship
and house of Henry's widow, the Queen Catherine
Parr. She wrote letters, of dutiful affection and
youthful piety, to her brother the King. The
small King, also learned, also devotional, sent
comfortable messages. Suddenly there fell upon
her a personal crisis, and one in no sense theological.

It was two years since the King had died. He
had been to the child a huge, terrifying, and
thrilling wonder ; all her life she recalled him,
a fabulous and yet familiar splendour. He was
her father, and he had put her mother to death ;
he had done so because, besides being her father,
he was also the King, and her mother had sinned
against the King in his kingdom. When she
called herself " Harry's daughter," the very
intimacy of the word increased the myth, and

she made herself more ordinary and more extraordinary at once. The child's imagination of him, being through his death undefeated by any natural conflict or scorn, matured, but it did not change its characteristics. She loved thrills, and this was the great thrill of her childhood. At sixteen she was provided with another. Catherine Parr married again, this time the brother of the Lord Protector, Thomas, Lord Seymour of Sudely.

Lord Seymour was one of the less contented lords of the Council. He was irked by what seemed to him the unnecessary greatness of his brother, and he had at first proposed to himself to make an even more royal alliance than with his new wife ; he thought of marrying Elizabeth herself. The Protector and the Council stopped him, and he fell back, at first secretly, on Catherine. In the triple household Elizabeth, maturing, sensuous, intellectual, found herself introduced to a new freedom, and to unprecedented freedoms. The Lord Seymour had a broad taste in jollity, and the Dowager Queen little inclination, at first, to discourage him. There were jests and romps. Elizabeth's room was visited in the early morning ; she was teased and tickled, mentally and corporally rolled and smacked. She was not alone in her experiences ; the other young ladies of the household also enjoyed the Lord Seymour's attentions. He

rollicked through his domestic world, as he attempted to rollick through his political. The
gardens of the house received the laughter of
the three great personages. The Princess was
held fast by the Dowager while Lord Seymour
cut up her skirt. Her education took a broad
scope, and presently, even in that world, caused
some scandal. Elizabeth was observed to blush
when the talk veered round to Seymour ; it was
suspected that she was beginning to be acutely
and unduly aware of him. The Queen Dowager
grew difficult and the household strained. Elizabeth eventually withdrew, in the spring of 1548,
thus re-establishing friendship with Catherine.
In the autumn the Dowager died. Elizabeth's
household were all for Seymour ; Elizabeth had
by no means forgotten him. Full life had
awakened in her. He returned to his hope of
marrying her ; meanwhile he had made himself
intimate with the young King. His head grew
full of visions of himself as Protector of the King
and husband of the Princess. He made vague
general preparations for something, and talked
more vaguely. He spoke of his brother as in-
tending to " enslave England by mercenaries."
In January 1549 the Council took action. He
was arrested. Immediately upon the news there
arrived from the Government deputies to cross-
examine the Princess. Members of her household found themselves under guard. Had there

been a plot? What did she know of the plot? Had she been in the plot? Into the full stirring of amorous excitement, however watched and warned it had been by her wary intelligence, there drove this sudden close catechism of peril. Her servants confessed all they knew, and perhaps more than she knew. Breathless, obstinate, betrayed to suspicion, besieged by threats, persuasions, and slanders, she denied " any practice." She wept in private and stormed in public. She was agitated over Seymour's imprisonment, but she stood staunchly to herself. Her exhausted examiners said she needed two governesses rather than one : " she hath a very good wit." Parry, her steward, testified that he had asked her if she would be willing to marry Seymour. She had answered, as anyone might, that " she could not tell her mind therein," but in her it was prophetic of the long series of replies in her future. It is not conceivable that Seymour could have roused in her any devotion of pure and superfluous self-sacrifice. The whole episode terminated by accentuating the necessity of a perpetual guard on her emotions and intelligence. There may have been also something of an angry contempt. It was clear that he had meant to use her. She probably knew it before ; now she felt it, and felt that others knew it.

They executed him. It was the second time the axe had swung near her life. Of her mother's death she knew only by reading and report, and there the figure of her mighty and monstrous father came between. She was sixteen now, and was left to her studies in Hatfield, peculiarly alone. Her sister Mary had more continuous difficulties, but Mary had the privilege, the peril, and the protection of a Cause and of a party, and of the attention of half Europe. Nothing except inconvenience hovered round Elizabeth. She retired into herself and her mind.

The lords continued intrigues. There were rebellions. The mercenaries marched – Hungarians against the Scotch, Germans and Italians against the men of Norwich and the men of the West Country. Certain of the Roman Catholic Italians afterwards sought absolution for having fought the battles of the heretic Protector ; the Lutheran Germans were less troubled in conscience. Somerset, having crushed the revolting peasants, tried to crush the rising power of the Dudleys, and failed. He was put to death. Dudley succeeded ; the King died ; Lady Jane Grey, married to Guildford Dudley, was proclaimed Queen. Dudley, now Duke of Northumberland, already at odds with Cranmer over Church doctrine and Church land, tried to raise the banner of the Reformed religion, and failed. Elizabeth, from wilfulness or wisdom, from principle or prudence, threw in her lot with her house and her sister. She came up to London

with a great following ; on the last day of July
1553 she rode out to meet the triumphant Mary.
She saluted and joined her. The daughter of
events rode into London next after the daughter
of metaphysic, two illegitimates. Into the city
of the Reformation rode the crowned champion
of the Counter-Reformation ; after her short,
thin figure, came the tall, handsome, and strik-
ing shape which was to be, in effect, both Counter-
Reformation and Counter-Counter-Reformation.
She was twenty, and she had learnt to keep her
mouth shut on her heart.

CHAPTER II

THE single danger to Elizabeth's person hitherto had been political ; now an element in which, by nature, she had no keen interest, entered her life : the element of dogma. The change upon the Throne had suddenly rendered herself and her household religiously suspect to the sovereign. Unless she could be converted she was bound to remain a precise threat of that permanent nature of heresy which was, in the period of the Reformation, its new and shattering characteristic. The two sisters, opposed in their theologies, were still more opposed in their temperaments. There was in Mary a strain of supernatural humility ; she devoutly and sincerely adored God and obeyed a revelation from God. There was in Elizabeth a queer strain of natural humility – or of that common sense which is unsanctified humility. She thought it was always quite possible that she might be wrong, and even more

26

strongly did she feel that everybody else might be wrong. When she was opposed or when she was angry, this natural humility was often lost in an equally natural obstinacy, but it existed. Mary exalted a hypothesis into faith – a superb and noble achievement. Elizabeth could hardly allow it to be even a hypothesis if she could not also feel that it was a fact. Elizabeth, expressing, after her own manner, her most sincere religious beliefs, would always have left Mary with a strong feeling that her sister was irreligious. Since, at present, from Mary's point of view, she was in matters of faith almost worse than irreligious, the hostility between them, bound at best to be subdued but permanent, grew to the worst and increased.

In a few months two things became clear. First, Mary's policy was to be actively and penally Roman ; second, she proposed to marry the Prince of Spain. The first was unpopular among the stalwarts of the true religion ; the second, almost everywhere. Spain was the great maritime commercial rival, the power threatening mastery. There was, if not a party, yet certainly a prejudice in favour of Elizabeth in two places – among the general populace of London and at the Court of France, both hostile to Spain. But Spain and Papalism were two separate things, and Elizabeth's immediate difficulty was with the second. For a few weeks she held aloof from the spreading triumph of the old Faith, but by the beginning of September she curtseyed to a great monarch. *Cujus regio, ejus religio* was a phrase which then beat in the heart ; nowadays it merely astonishes the brain. The Princess contemplated the restored rites ; she considered her sister's awful will, and it is to be remembered that the will of the sovereign meant a very great deal then. She considered her own position also ; eventually she asked for instruction. She went to Mass – not too often. The mistrustful Mary made inquiries of her ; the Princess protested the honesty of her devotion. The Queen remained suspicious both of her sister's spectacular beauty and her sister's spectacular behaviour. But she knew she owed goodwill to Elizabeth as to all of God's creatures ; she laboured to be intelligent and yet to pay her debt.

Her careful mind, a little taking after the legalism of her father Henry, proceeded to take steps to repeal the statute which declared her own illegitimacy ; Elizabeth's, naturally, she left explicitly untouched. But she went farther. She thought Elizabeth, being a legal and canonical bastard, ought not to reign. The Queen therefore desired to repeal that other statute, which set Anne Boleyn's daughter in the way of the succession. She was warned that it would prove impossible, and, thwarted in her logic, she grew less capacious in goodwill. The first political results of the new religious revival, of the faith which was pressed upon her, exhibited to Elizabeth a loss of her future right to the Throne and a growing personal antagonism. She answered as well as she could. She did her best to hover interestingly at the gate of the Roman fold ; at that personal cost she could not want to enter, but she had no desire to be left to the dangers of the wilderness. It was not only her physical danger in, but her intellectual distaste for, the wilderness that revolted her. She did not much care for the fierce company of the extreme Reforming fanatics who wandered there. She did not want to go anywhere, yet it seemed she, first of all England, must make a public, responsible decision to go somewhere – credally. She was the Queen's sister and successor ; it was impossible that she should not be a marked person. Cranmer and others were out of favour and soon to be in prison ; Cecil and others were out of favour and living in retirement – Cecil himself discreetly going to Mass after the old style. She fell from favour. In November the Lady Elizabeth asked permission to withdraw from the Court. It was granted. On her way out of London, five hundred gentlemen in her train, she sent a message to the Queen asking for a supply of vestments. It is by no means certain that she was not sincere, in her own way.

She was not drawn to the Roman party by conscience, but neither was she conscientiously
opposed. Nothing was more remote from her
conscience than the whole ecclesiastical problem.
Only she did not love yielding to threats, and to
her of all people in the realm the doctrine came
accompanied by implicit threats. She did not
mind a pretence at a readiness to surrender.
But a pretence of readiness to surrender is not
quite a pretence of surrender – not quite the
same to the actor and not quite the same to the
spectator. It was this delicate distinction which
caused uneasiness in her sister, her servants, and
her enemies ; it was this distinction which be-
wildered her contemporaries throughout her life.

At the beginning of January 1554 ambassadors
came from the Emperor to settle the affair of
the Queen's marriage ; at the end, rebellion
broke out in Kent and elsewhere. Sir Thomas
Wyatt led a march on London. He was defeated
by the measures and the ardour of the Queen,
and as soon as his defeat was accomplished
orders were sent that Elizabeth should be brought
back to London for examination. She was very
unwilling to go ; she said she was ill, which was
at any rate partly true. She said she was innocent and ignorant, which is not so likely. A
letter of hers had been found in the dispatches
of the French ambassador. She and the ambassador both swore vehemently that it was not

hers. There was evidence that letters had been
written to her by Wyatt ; she swore she had
received none, and none from her to Wyatt
could be found. The Imperial ambassador was
pressing for her execution. The anti-Spanish
party in the Council resisted him, and he wrote
to his master complaining of their obstruction.
The Queen, who was not only religious but also
moral, would do nothing unjustified by morals
and law. The balance swung almost level.

Elizabeth came to London. In an open litter,
very pale, very haughty, in extreme danger,
she passed through the streets. Three weeks
afterwards further orders against her were given ;
she was to be conveyed to the Tower. It was
Palm Sunday, and a rainy day, when the barge
received her – during the time of Mass, when
the streets would be least peopled. At Traitor's
Gate, as she landed, she became, for the first
recorded time, her public self. She stood still ;
she looked up to the dark skies ; she cried :
" Lord, I never thought to come here as prisoner."
She turned from heaven to the people ; she
called out to the guards around her : " I pray
you all, good friends and fellows, bear me witness
that I come in no traitor, but as true a woman
to the Queen's Majesty as any now living, and
thereon will I take my death."

Nothing quite sufficient against her could be
found to put in evidence, though the Lord

Chancellor Gardiner was suspected of suppressing a packet of letters. Division in the Council, agitation in London, Wyatt's dying declaration that she was innocent, made it impossible for Mary to act, even if she wished. In spite of the Imperial ambassador, Elizabeth was released in May, and dispatched to the honourable semicaptivity in which, now less and now more guarded, she was to remain. It was an experience not without an effect on her future years and acts ; if she were so detained and watched, so might other royal persons properly be. She had inconvenient friends ; so other royalties might have. For the moment she breathed delight. She was sent, in the custody of Sir Henry Bedingfield, to Woodstock, making slow time, and turning the journey almost into a pastoral progress. Guns of salute were fired in London, bells rung in the country. Villagers cheered her, thronged round her, brought her presents. She came laughing through the country roads ; she was not yet twenty-one. At Woodstock she remained for a year, watched, but left free to her personal tastes, even in religion. The Roman devotion of her earlier interest was for awhile abandoned ; she used – by permission – the English service. Her intellectual exploration had ceased, but the chance of things had thrown her with the New Learning and the Reforming party, and they with her.

They had, both parties, nowhere else to look, though neither was quite at ease *tali auxilio*. She made herself as tiresome to the unfortunate Sir Henry Bedingfield as a young woman of a restless, provocative, cautious, witty, and intelligent temper could, but they remained good friends. She tried to sound – possibly she even tried to be – simple and honest to her sister, but Mary thoroughly distrusted her. With reason ; Elizabeth was not by nature simple, and never succeeded in convincing anybody that she was. Honesty is another matter. She did not believe in a number of things, yet she was not quite clear that she disbelieved. In the intervals she attended to the small events about her. There was Sir Henry to provoke, young men to tease, and the fields and the people to enjoy. She let herself enjoy.

In London the preparations for the marriage with the Spaniard, and for the reconciliation with the Roman See, went on, not without difficulty between the two movements. The Prince Philip, created King of Naples by his father, landed in July ; trains of Spanish gentlemen and soldiers paraded the capital. Philip, anxious to conform to English customs, drank ale. The formal marriage took place on 25 July. Mary became, then or later, by the grace of God, " quene of Englande, Spaine, Fraunce, both Sicilles, Jerusalem, and Ireland. Archduchesse

CE

of Austria, Duchesse of Burgundy, Myllane, and
Brabant.   Countesse of Hapsburge, Flanders,
and Tyroll." In November the Lord Reginald
Pole, Cardinal-Deacon of St. Mary Cosmedin,
came up the Thames in the royal barge, a silver
cross shining at its prow ; the fortunate tide
swept him, an hour before his time, to Whitehall.
The King and Queen received him, Philip saying, " We will place the Queen between us " ;
the Legate turned a sentence ; the Queen
lamented the delay ; the Legate brought the
salutations to a climax by saying that the Lord
had delayed him till now he could say, " Beatus
fructus ventris tui." Five days later the Houses
drew up a petition to the King and Queen, im-
ploring reconciliation with the Roman See ; one
member of the Commons spoke, and one more
voted, in contradiction. On 30 November it
was presented in the palace. The Lord Cardinal
pronounced the absolution over the kneeling
Houses. Within a few days they made more
complete amends. They corrected legal heresy
by reintroducing the old laws, and they created
" an Act repealing all statutes, articles, and pro-
visions made against the See Apostolic of Rome
since the twentieth year of King Henry the
Eighth, and also for the establishment of all
spiritual and ecclesiastical possessions and heredi-
taments conveyed to the laity." In spite, however, of this last determination, which was

unpalatable to the Queen, to the Legate, and to the Apostolic See itself, the great new ordering of England had been achieved. The realm stood with Spain and those other scattered dominions of the royal title in the front of the Counter-Reformation. Not only Spain and England, but also France, rejoiced ; thanksgivings were offered there in the churches. The champions of the Henrican formulation were converted – either honestly, like Gardiner, or dishonestly, like Cecil – or they were in prison or in danger of prison, like Cranmer. It seemed as if Europe were returning to its basis of philosophical unity. The great alliance awaited but one event to ratify it – the birth of an heir, which should make of no importance the unreliable religious mutations of the Lady Elizabeth.

She was not converted, like Gardiner ; she was not in prison, like Cranmer ; she was not quite conforming, like Cecil. She never would or she never could go quite far enough to be convincing. Interpretations of Elizabeth's character, especially at this time, turn always on how much there was in her of *would not* and how much of *could not*. That slender, swaying, unfixable division, in a Gallio-like mind sustaining a royal and sensuous body, the more avid of life that it was often liable to illness, is the mark upon which so much judgement has turned. But if her exact belief was, and is, uncertain, the implications of

that belief were certain.   Once she accepted, in
her soul, the Roman obedience, that moment
she would admit, to her soul and to the world,
her canonical and legal illegitimacy.   She would
deny the validity of her mother's marriage ; she
would deny, publicly and profoundly, the justice
of her claim to the Crown.   To hint at the denial
of those things to others, in interviews or
audiences, might be possible to her ; it was not
possible that she should deny them to herself.
No woman ever possessed in a greater degree
than Elizabeth that great feminine capacity for
identifying her personal desires with righteous-
ness and her personal needs with the justice of
God.

She abandoned the English service for the
Latin ; she renewed her religious flirtation with
the old Order that was now the new.   The pressure of events drove her more and more into a
waiting on events.   In 1555 she had another
interview with the Queen by night at Hampton
Court. The Queen, incredulously desiring justice,
half-blamed, half-interrogated her sister.   " You
stand stoutly on your truth ; I pray God it may
so fall out."   The Princess answered with as-
severations ; if they were all true, it remained
that her life and her temper of mind were, merely
in themselves and without action, hostile to
Mary's desire.   The Queen accused her of thinking and saying that she had been punished

unjustly. The Princess answered, " No, if it please your Majesty, I have borne the burden and must bear it." In a sense other than that of wardship and imprisonment she bore the burden – the fetters of illegitimacy, the phantasmal flicker of the Crown.

For by now a change had taken place in the Court, and, as time passed and the course of nature produced no heir, that change became more marked. There was division, not only between orthodoxy and heresy, but in the whole front of Papal orthodoxy itself. The chief division was between Spain and France. The King became aware that, if his wife had no child, and if Elizabeth did not succeed, then the Throne would fall to the next heir, who was Mary of Scotland, the great-granddaughter of Henry VII. But Mary of Scotland was to be married to the Dauphin Francis of France, and then her accession would make one empire of France, Scotland, and England. It was a question in his mind whether the triumph of Catholicism were worth the triumph of France. He decided that it was not ; perhaps to his orthodox eyes the union of the considerable heretical minority in France with the suppressed heretical minority in England seemed dangerous. The process of politics defeated his religious passion. He was compelled to compromise – in his statecraft, if not in his soul – and it was his misfortune that he had to compromise on Elizabeth, who by this time was rapidly becoming an incarnate variation of compromise. He did for his policy what she did for her life : he fell in with the situation. The Spanish influence at Court was thrown on the side of Elizabeth's preservation and dignity. Better heresy and illegitimacy, which might be converted or subdued, than Catholicism and France, which would be secularly hostile.

It is part of the fantasy of politics that at the same time efforts were being made, with French help, to overthrow Mary and put Elizabeth on the Throne. It seemed wiser to the French ambassador to establish her than to run the serious risk of the birth of a child or the uncertain attempt to impose Mary of Scotland. In the autumn of 1555 a plot was discovered by the Government ; in Elizabeth's London house was found a mass of seditious books. Half a dozen of her servants were arrested, but she herself was not touched. The influence of Philip was decisive. The Queen wrote kindly to her ; she devotionally answered. The most that was done was to put her again under some sort of wardship. Her household was said " to lead a licentious life, especially in matters of religion," and Sir Thomas Pope was sent down to oversee it. In a combination of morals and metaphysics the loose behaviour of her subordinate Court was to be trimmed by more rigorous discipline.

A more serious danger to her – a danger that could only be avoided by dexterity and obstinacy – was enforced marriage. It had once been proposed to marry her to a great English noble, William Courtenay ; but Courtenay died in 1556. Philip was anxious to marry her to his ally, the Duke of Savoy, thus providing her with a Roman Catholic husband and himself with a secure England. She was urged ; she refused. She was warned by her friends that it was proposed to marry her and carry her over to Flanders ; she said she would die rather than go. The efforts to impose the discipline of marriage upon her failed as the efforts to impose the discipline of Roman doctrine had failed. The goodwill of France, the goodwill of Spain, the goodwill of the Reformers, all swayed on to her side. She did not conceive that she owed gratitude to any of them. In 1558 the Queen desired once more to strike her from the succession, and was again defeated. Philip declined to agree. He claimed some credit afterwards, which Elizabeth only accorded when she wanted to placate him. In herself she gave the credit to her God and her own mind.

As if events hurried to help her, there came to England the news of the fall of Calais. The French war had been entered upon not entirely for the sake, but under the influence, of Philip. The shock of the capture of a city which had been

English for centuries struck far. All discontent,
religious and political, looked to Elizabeth. The
year passed in fevers and famines, with labour-
ing finances and amid the last executions. The
executions under Mary, as those later under
Elizabeth, were nominally the business of the
State for the preservation of the State, as executions for heresy always had been. They were
not frequent or unusual enough to cause any
violent increase of popular anger, but at least
they did not lessen popular discontent. In 1558
forty died ; the last five at Canterbury, on
10 November, when the Queen already lay
dying. By then loyalty to Elizabeth had become
fashionable. She was no curmudgeon ; she proceeded to enjoy it. Sir William Cecil removed
to Hatfield to be near her – the first arrival of
the Cecils at Hatfield. The Court followed.
Mary demanded, before she would sanction the
passage of the Crown to her half-sister, a promise
to maintain Roman Catholic doctrine. Elizabeth was neither cruel nor conscientious ; what
she had done for herself she did for Mary. At
that late hour it was unnecessary, for nothing
could prevent her accession. Her answer does
not remain ; it seems she gave her promise.
Mary sank into a semi-delirium. The attention
of all Europe was fixed on Hatfield. As if the
order Mary had established was also passing,
thirteen bishops within a year preceded or

followed the Queen in death. On 17 November, in that almost Oriental magnificence of priestly escort, Mary died.

The Lady Elizabeth received the news at Hatfield. She was twenty-five years old. On the gold sovereigns that she was to coin she retained the inscription set there by Mary : *a Domino factum est, et est mirabile in oculis nostris.* *Mirabile* she remained ; *factum est Domino* is disputed.

CHAPTER III

AT the time of the Queen's accession the division
of Europe upon the nature of the visible Church
had been for some time accepted as a temporary
fact. It was a fact which neither side hoped or
feared or supposed could be permanent. It was
expressed in two definite events : the Diet and
Confession of Augsburg (1555) and the Council
of Trent (1545–63). The one had determined at
least the right of the Protesting Churches to
supremacy in any State where the sovereign was
Protestant ; the other, correcting the decrees of
the Council of Constance, was defining the re-
forms in action and doctrine of the Papal Church.
At Constance the Council had decided between
the conflicting claimants to Rome, and had
asserted its formal superiority to the See. At
Trent the Legates of the Pope controlled the
Council, and virtually established the supernatural autocracy which later was to be more

exactly defined by the Pope himself in the Infallibility decree of 1870. The Conciliar movement within the bounds of the Papal Church was left to become the threat of the Kings ; before the end of that century it had been perpended in France and proposed in Spain, so uncertain yet was the Pastorate of Rome.

In 1560 the suspended Council was resummoned. The expectation of the Churches and nations protesting against the See of Rome was that its decisions would be followed by combined Catholic action to destroy all of them – or at least heresy in all of them, which might mean the same thing. The Pope entertained a hope to the same effect ; fire and sword were to restore unity. He was willing, however, that they should first express their views. Their divines could not, naturally, sit on the Council and vote, but they might address it and argue before it. It was as far as he could possibly go – that may be conceded ; but it must be conceded also that such a position would be (except by such faith in a miracle as Christ seems to discourage) impossible for Protestant divines. It was determined in England that Anglican bishops should not attend.

It was not, however, the gathering at Trent which had defeated the progress of the Reformation so much as the new spiritual energy which inspired Rome and her champions. Holy and

austere souls now shone round the Lateran on
the Cœlian Hill ; the Jesuits were founded in
1534 and approved in 1540 as peculiar missionaries of the Church ; the Inquisition, as the
Holy Office, was universally established as a
means of purgation in 1541. The supreme utility
of sanctity lay at the disposal of the victorious
Papacy ; names, now of world-wide invocation,
had then the meaning of men in streets and
houses. Ignatius Loyola, John D'Avila, Francis
Xavier, Francis Borgia, Teresa, Philip Neri,
Charles Borromeo – these and others intensified
the power and lustre of the Roman cause. In
1558 it did not seem unlikely that the whole of
Christendom would be recovered by the Roman
See, in spite of the difficulties and disputes which
continually arose between that See and the Kings
of France and Spain, and between those Kings
themselves. Yet in fact something other than
those bitter but domestic quarrels was to emerge
– a spirit, a quality of mind, which may be called
scepticism or realism or toleration or cynicism or
wisdom according to the kind of mind which
possesses it ; perhaps, making allowance for her
femininity, perversity, obstinacy, and fear, it might
be called Elizabethan. It was the spirit which
puts the supernatural in its place, a habit which,
losing much, gains something, and without which
religion is only tolerable in and by saints. At
least that spirit, like her own, is flagrant in its

egotism, and neither cares nor is able to conceal
its own limited and earthly nature by borrowing
glory from a vast universal religion ; so far its
honesty is manifest. A worldly hypocrite Elizabeth might be ; she never succeeded in being a
religious. Nor, at bottom, did she desire it ;
her refusal continually betrayed her hypocrisies
to a perhaps not much less hypocritical world.
It separated her from the Minister who stood by
her, who piously defended his pious frauds. Yet
Cecil too had his sincerity ; it was in his perfect
realization of himself as an official and Civil
Servant. If Mary had had an heir, Cecil might
easily have remained Catholic – he had been one
of the gentlemen sent by Mary to meet Philip of
Spain in Flanders – and might still, though with
more difficulty, become Treasurer. He could
not keep away from business ; he never failed
in it ; he never illumined it.

For forty years Elizabeth and he worked
together ; of old it was generally supposed for
good, now it is as generally, and as fashionably,
supposed for harm. They were intimate, and
intimately dependent. Yet perhaps neither of
them ever quite trusted the other, and each of
them a little despised the other, working rather
better for that element of comforting contempt.
They both hid secrets. Cecil deliberately concealed facts ; the Queen, less deliberately, her
heart. She chose him rather than he her, and for

his capacity, especially a capacity which had ensured not only self-preservation but occupation both under Edward and Mary. It is more likely that she understood him than he her. The mind of a woman is mysterious ; so, it is said, is the heart of a Prince.

Cecil was her supporter ; over the seas, in France, was one who wished to be her supplanter. As soon as Mary Tudor was dead, Mary Queen of Scots, wife of the Dauphin of France, quartered the royal arms of England on her own, and thus proclaimed to the world the illegitimacy and usurpation of the Queen of England. According to Roman Catholic ecclesiastical order she was undoubtedly justified. The exact position of a sovereign who, theologically incompetent of succession by birth, is yet legally nominated to the succession by a previous occupant, was a question for the legalists, whom it occupied. Except for Mary Stuart, illegitimacy would have been mostly a term of abuse ; given Mary, it was a threat and a danger, for it meant Mary. Yet at the moment Mary, to England, was only a name.

In the dark closing days of November the young Queen came to London, and made processions – coming to Charterhouse on 23 November, riding to the Tower five days later, going by water to Somerset House a week after, and finally, on 23 December, moving to Whitehall. She played for the popularity she loved, and won it. Now she was free to deal with men and women under no suspicious eyes and in no danger of hostile reports. She had not been so free for eleven years, and before that she had been but a child. The crowds roared round her, and she smiled at them ; they shouted at her, and she decorously jested back. They brought her little bunches of flowers, and she accepted them ; they made Latin speeches to her, and she understood them. Every spectacle was a harmony of joy ; she keyed it up to a higher and higher pitch by her own delight. The Most High and Mighty Princess Elizabeth, by the grace of God, etc., etc., etc., had come to her city – to the ostentation, the cheering, the populace.

On Sunday, 15 January, 1559, she was crowned at Westminster, having had more processions and welcomes during the preceding days. In Westminster Hall the bishops, coped and mitred, received her. She came ; she was censed ; the Archbishop of York and another bishop gave her holy water and the Pax. They all sang *Salve, festa dies*, and the procession moved on, along layers of purple cloth, to the Abbey. She exhibited herself to the people, and was acclaimed. Mass was said. She was anointed, and crowned by the Bishop of Carlisle.

There had been at that Coronation Mass one small point of alteration : the Host had not been elevated after consecration. What was more, the

alteration had been at the Queen's own instructions, for the same thing had occurred in the royal
chapel a few weeks before. There she had been
disobeyed, and it was reported that she had risen
and left the chapel. Or, as some said, she had
ordered the celebrant not to elevate, and he had
answered that he must, and so she had left at the
end of the Gospel. It was even reported that at
the Coronation there was no consecration at all,
which is nonsense. The certain thing is that
neither in the chapel nor in the Abbey was there
elevation. It was a point immaterial ; it did not
directly concern doctrine but ritual. Nevertheless it was doubly significant. There were various
hypotheses concerning the mode of the Presence
in the Sacrament. One – to speak roughly –
held that a Presence of Christ existed at the
moment of reception ; one at the moment of
consecration. The first had been held by
Cranmer and others ; the second was orthodox at
Rome. There was also the hypothesis that the
Real Presence was in no sense intervolved with
the bread and wine ; that belonged to the more
extreme Reforming bodies. It was arguable that
the Queen's action was insignificant ; that it
affected no doctrine. But if it affected any, it
affected the Roman. It withdrew from the
public declaration of the Roman hypothesis
concerning the mode of the Presence ; it did no
more. It was the exact symbol of all Elizabeth's

religious acts at the beginning. Even the Acts of
Parliament that followed in 1559 – only five years
after the superb Reconciliation – did not commit
her to more than a kind of inconvenient silence
towards Rome. The lands that Mary had
restored to the Church were given back to the
Crown, on the plea of necessity ; the monasteries
refounded by Mary were also made over to the
Crown. The Queen's Majesty was declared the
only Supreme Governor – she refused " Supreme
Head " – " as well in all ecclesiastical things
or causes as temporal." Foreign jurisdiction,
princely or prelatic, was renounced. But no
direct mention was made of the Pope ; indeed,
in the last clause of one Bill a particular appeal
to Rome on a marriage cause was allowed – on
condition that Rome gave answer within sixty
days. The Queen withdrew, but that was
expected ; she withdrew only to a degree, and
that at least was to the good. She became
ambiguous, and that was merely perplexing. But
the Spanish ambassador made allowances ; she
was but a girl, quick but imprudent.

There was dancing at Whitehall. The Queen
was twenty-five and free, and the mistress of a
Court of Renascence gentlemen, who all wrote
poetry and made music and kissed hands and lips,
and flaunted their colours and flashed their
swords. Courtesies rose into compliments, compliments into flatteries, flatteries into the wildest

DE

flights of amorous verbal rapture. The Queen
enjoyed language, and the more dangerously
passionate the language the more she enjoyed it.
She delighted in cerebral adoration, and the
stronger the hint of corporal madness the more
she delighted in it. She had a supreme and
unfair advantage ; she was the Queen. She was
entirely safe in her person, even from incivility,
except in a decent pretence of despair. Her
servants' favours, their fortunes, their freedom,
their very lives, depended on her. She could
flash a look that struck the rashest courtier into
terror, and what any woman might attempt in
arrogance of femininity the power of England
lay behind to encourage and protect. If any
authority existed to which she would bend, it
must be an authority as profound as the freedom
and royalty in her which had been the result of
so many years' bitter awareness. She danced and
dined and rode and revelled, and all around her
and her few ladies circled Euphuistic adoration.
" The Queen is by nature of a high spirit," wrote
the Venetian ambassador in 1560, " and has
become more so owing to her good fortune, and
the many physical and mental endowments
which she possesses, so she has lofty designs, and
promises herself success in all of them."

She had promised herself success. It was universally assumed that she must have a husband to
ensure it. It was also realized that her husband –

that is, her marriage – would, directly or in-
directly, determine the particular scheme of
metaphysics and pattern of politics with which
she would accord : Romanism and France, or
Romanism and Spain, or Protestantism and
England, or even (though less probably) Romanism and England. A foreign marriage might not
be popular, but it might be necessary ; only by
such subordination to one of the Great Powers
could the small nation on their sea frontiers be
preserved from conquest. At the moment the
small nation was at war with France – or, rather,
negotiating peace with France under the slightly
detached assistance of Spain. The chief desire of
the English was the recovery of Calais. Without
the help of King Philip they were hardly likely
to get it.

Philip, a little slowly, and under the propulsion
of his ambassador in England, came to a conclusion. The settlement of Europe – that is, the
establishment of Roman order and the diplomatic defeat of the French monarchy – could be
best served, he had known for years, by the
satisfactory settlement in marriage of the Queen
of England. The Queen was coyly reluctant to
accept any of his nominees. He determined on a
grand gesture ; he offered her himself. She must,
of course, be converted ; " in this way it will be
evident I am serving the Lord by marrying her."
He did not anticipate much difficulty. He felt,

without perhaps admitting it to his conscientious
mind, that she would think her kingdom worth
a Mass. So she might have done – apart from
Philip – if the old difficulty had not recurred : in
order to gain a kingdom that way, she must first
acknowledge that she had no right to it in any
way. The Pope offered olive-branches : let her
submit and all should be forgiven. Let her admit
that she was a bastard and she should be treated
as a Queen. Let her admit that she was a
bastard – and as an inevitable corollary that the
other woman who in Paris magnificently flaunted
the arms of England was justified, was rightful
Queen – let her admit that, and she might perhaps keep the Crown as a Papal or Spanish gift.
Let her admit that she was a supplanter and she
might be permitted to reign. Elizabeth was the
last woman in the world to take refuge from
another woman under the protection of a priest
or of a husband. The King of Spain did not
believe that she could maintain at once the show
of right and the fact of rule. She believed that
she could. Her emotional imagination maintained that she was that strange and superb thing,
Harry's daughter, and Harry's daughter was
Queen of England, and England was rapturous
to have her. She had spent years defending her
life and her freedom – such as it was – with all
the resources of her intelligence. It did not seem
to her much of a sin to use the same resources to

maintain independently the Crown she had independently achieved. She set herself to deal with events, unencouraged and unhampered by metaphysics, and (it must be admitted) by morals. It did not seem to her that her morals were less just, in their way, than those which marked the progress of her metaphysical and royal rivals. Her femininity assisted her ; she hurled herself into her lack of pattern with as much ardour as other women – her sister Mary, for example – had hurled themselves into patterns, and her energy and her capacity in that motion were a principal element in the exclusion of philosophy from the councils of Europe.

Ambassadors and suits of marriage thronged her – from Scotland, from France, from Sweden, from the Empire, from Spain. She showed willingness to them all, but Philip had been the first, and Philip's adventure was over before the others had well begun. His ambassador had written that he would " pick to pieces one by one those whom she might marry here." The ambassador talked ; she responded, but she dallied. She said she was not inclined to marry. She said that to marry her sister's widower would be to insult the memory of her father, who had conscientiously put away his brother's widow. In fact, though the comment was not serious, the underlying fact was : to marry him would be once more to advertise her illegitimacy. She said she could not marry him, for she was a heretic. She did not seem to grasp that she need not go on being a heretic. She suggested that they might go on being friends. In April, Philip caused the proposal to be withdrawn. Elizabeth, between sighs and smiles, lamented to the ambassador that his master could not be much in love if he would not wait four months. It had not occurred to Philip or to the ambassador that he was, or was supposed to be. The Queen went on dancing to the thrilling notes of the cerebralized passion of the Court, and all the immediate marriage possibilities slid slowly by into the past. To the Commons, urging marriage, she had cerebralized virginity ; she became almost lyrical over the marble sepulchre that should proclaim how a Queen had lived and died a virgin. In fact the phrase objectifies what was by now an inevitable element in her nature – her vigil, her self-determination, her self-preservation. The marble stone with its epitaph symbolized them ; so virgin, so buried, so gloriously famed as a beneficent sovereign to her people, she was indeed secure. Virginity in past times had been a vocation ; she spoke of it so, but indeed in her speech it had changed its nature. Evitable or inevitable, it was already no more than an event.

Amid the thrilling and important concerns of love and religion was another, hardly less important, and, to Elizabeth's mind, hardly less

thrilling – money. The finances of the country –
that is to say, of the Crown, for in most matters
all national expenses were the expenses of the
Crown ; subjects did not expect to have to pay –
had been for years in a very improper state.
Elizabeth and Cecil were in this at one. They
set to work to re-establish credit, at home and
abroad. The expenditure of the Court was reduced. Tax returns were investigated, currency
was improved – base coins called in, and a smaller
proportion of good issued. The Queen, unex-
pectedly, made a profit ; trade was assisted.
Money was sent abroad to pay off foreign debts.
Her credit went up and up. All her life she
worked at that reserve of strength. Her rhetoric
was cut upon the stone of her economy, which was
as hard to be moved as the imaginary lid of that
other sepulchre which, in her rhetoric, she pre-
destined for her grave. Money also she treated
as a series of events, and no dogma could persuade
her to loosen those events. There is in this a
peculiar and satisfying likeness between her and
that greater spirit, already close on birth, which
was to be the chief glory of her reign ; nor did the
mind of Shakespeare, when it ceased from *Othello*,
forget to use reasonable means to recover his
proper dues from his debtor at Stratford. The
English, a nation of shopkeepers, are a nation of
poets, of whom a number of the best came literally
out of shops. They, like the angel of the

Apocalypse, set one foot on the known and one on the unknown ; it is their balance, and Elizabeth and Shakespeare in their different ways are two of those who kept it.

Meanwhile, as those first months drew into years, the Queen's more general appetite for enjoyment, without losing much of its general scope, distinguished a particular opportunity. The first Favourite arose. Favourites were general through Europe in that age, and not only general but public. They were public figures as Favourites ; the very name was used without any sense of degradation. It was no more shameful to be the Prince's Favourite than to be a Minister or Secretary ; often the Favourite was used as a Minister, and had to work as hard. He was, however, peculiarly the Prince's intimate ; his whole glory, his substantial being, under heaven, depended on the Prince's personal liking. He was apt to be a difficulty to the normal diplomats. There arose, shining in her favour, at the Court of Elizabeth, the figure of Lord Robert Dudley, son of that Northumberland who had attempted to establish a dynasty. The Queen and he had been friends in youth, and friends under Mary. On her accession he had been made Master of the Horse.

He appeared now, rising in the Court and presently in the Council, portentous of the Queen's personal delights and desires, distinguished by her femininity beyond all his fellows. It even began to

seem as if that grand inscription on the marble
sepulchre would never have a chance to get itself
cut.   Nobody had taken her protestations of a
virginal future very seriously ; at twenty-six, in
the throb of a new life, women might talk so.   It
was but a spectacular event, that day when the
young Queen proclaimed that her life was to be
dedicated to the motherhood of her people.   Less
spectacular incidents were reported in 1559 ; the
Queen was said to visit Lord Robert's lodgings by
night.   It was said that if his wife died – she was
ill of cancer – Elizabeth would marry him.   The
ambassadors wrote of it, and the common people
gossiped.   The Court grew busy with scandal and
some anger.   Dudley was of no such high birth
or grand estate that he could be easily contemplated as a master.   The Queen made him all but
master, yet if ever he presumed upon what she
had given she struck him back.   " I will have here
but one mistress, and no master," she swore, and
that one at least of her many oaths she kept.

The days ran on into 1560, to the autumn.
There were many subjects of anxiety – the Pope,
Spain, Scotland, France.   Even yet, as September came, the existence of the Queen seemed
strange ; the lords of Europe momently expected
something to happen – conversion or rebellion,
marriage or assassination.   She was still a *lusus
naturæ*, a thing that could not last.   Suddenly a
new wave of an outrageous rumour swept over

Europe. Lady Robert Dudley had been found dead in her country house. It was universally suspected that her husband had slain her – Cecil had hinted as much to the Spanish ambassador on the previous day – and that the Queen had been passive accomplice. This, it was said in France, was the fruit of heresy ; the English ambassador heard the taunt at the Court where Mary Stuart dwelt, ignorant yet of Darnley and Bothwell and Kirk o' Field. The shocked ambassadors, writing frantically home, received small comfort from Cecil, who, while Dudley throve, stood in need of some comfort himself. Hearts almost stood still ; would the Queen take the last fatal step ? Would she marry her – paramour ?

For a while it looked as if she would. The coroner's jury declared a death by misadventure ; another inquiry found no other conclusion. Dudley was officially innocent ; the more, she. As opinion in England settled, she fell away from what in the one wild moment of crisis had seemed possible. The danger over, and nothing having happened – beyond Amy Robsart's death – she became irritable. In November, Dudley was on the point of being raised to the peerage. The patent was made out ; they brought it her. She slashed it with a penknife, with a bitter reference to the treachery of the dead Dudleys. Then she became kind again. Cecil swung back into favour, and then again out, but, in favour or out,

he stuck to his job and she kept him at it. It was
the one certain thing on which they were agreed.
Through the growing winter of 1560 and longer
the uncertainty lasted. In December a foreign
event changed Europe : Francis, King of France,
husband of Mary Stuart, died. Mary was deprived of a kingdom and even of influence in it,
for with the new King the influence of Catherine
de Medici became paramount. Mary's attention turned vividly to her own kingdom in the
north.

During the years 1559 and 1560, while Elizabeth had been receding from Rome, manœuvring
about marriage, reforming the finance, figuring
in public scandal with Lord Robert, and, above
all, manipulating the public spectacle of her own
imagination of herself as Harry's daughter and
Queen of England, she had been forced also,
rather against her will, into activity in Scotland.
There, as in the rest of Europe, metaphysical and
political schisms ran varyingly criss-cross. The
Calvinist and local Lords of the Congregation
had attacked the Catholic and European Regent
in Leith, a Guise princess, widow of James V,
and Mary's mother. Elizabeth had no wish –
she never had – to assist rebellion, especially
Protestant rebellion, but she had no wish that the
French armies of the Regent and her daughter
should control Scotland, " the postern-gate " of
England. In their hands the gate would be far

too convenient an entry for Roman and Marian invasion ; she herself would become more dependent than ever for her safety on the goodwill of the King of Spain. If she and the national mass which she thought to control and express were to swing free in their own orbit, she must keep it from the influence of both of the two great planets ; that is, as far as possible, she must keep Scotland subordinate to her own influence. Since the Queen of Scotland in Paris was flaunting the English royal arms, Elizabeth felt herself the freer to interfere, without any flaunting of the interference, with the royal arms of Scotland. Neither to herself nor to the other members of the European guild of monarchs did she wish to admit that she was doing so. At no exact point could she be brought to admit that acts of war were being committed. She did not like war for many reasons : it was expensive ; it was wasteful also of lives, and she was never one, unless greatly moved, to like spending lives any more than money ; finally, it tended to be a decisive crisis, and all her involuntary training had brought her to dislike decisive crises. She had known too many and too dangerous. But when a crisis forced itself on her, she could act as if she had hastened to meet it. She did not hasten to this one. English money appeared in the camp of the Lords of the Congregation, English ships in the Firth of Forth. Their hovering neutrality flowered in hostile acts against the French. Protests to the Queen produced only astonishment, incredulity, demands for more and more particulars, expositions of the impossibility of disciplinary action on the admiral without exacter knowledge. The Spanish ambassador secretly encouraged Cecil, who was much more pro-war than his mistress, being much more Protestant. Any damage to the French suited Philip's schemes of policy. He wanted neither heresy victorious nor Mary triumphant, and his compromising diplomacy lay tendentiously behind the young Queen, who was certainly not Mary and might eventually not be heretical. At Rome his representatives exhorted the Pope to patience.

Domestic troubles multiplied in France and Spain. The permissible moment for open war arrived. The Queen allowed an English army to appear in the Lords' camp before Leith. Everyone thought it very wrong, but no one was in an immediate position to interfere. The Queen had a hand in the triumph of the Lords' party and gained a voice in the negotiation. In July 1560 the Treaty of Edinburgh was concluded, subject to ratification. By it, not only were the French to withdraw from Scotland, but Francis and Mary were to cease from bearing Elizabeth's blazon and claiming Elizabeth's Throne. It was the first definite phenomenon of Elizabeth victorious, the first imposition of herself as an indubitable fact on dynastic and dogmatic Europe. The Lords of the Congregation rejoiced metaphysically, as if the treaty were a theological definition. To Elizabeth it was a personal event. She was urged by her Ministers to spend money on the Lords; she consistently refused. She imposed her economy at home while imposing her reputation abroad – two sides of the spectacle which was Elizabeth.

At one point – and that the most important – she failed. She could not force the treaty on Mary Stuart, who merely refused to ratify it and continued to embroider her actual throne with the symbols of her potential. The scandal of Cumnor Hall in September encouraged her. The shocked horror of Elizabeth and Mary at each other's marital or non-marital adventures is not the least among the bitter-sweets of history. The refusal of ratification made of a political a personal quarrel; it fretted Elizabeth in the tender spot of her political relation to her father Henry, and combined with that a minor irritation on the question of orthodoxy. Elizabeth's religious emotions, by her nature perhaps but also by her early circumstances, were inextricably involved with her personal and patriotic, and they also together. Her character had been formed too early under the threat of violence; her unity lay in her idea of herself, and she suffered the disadvantage of that premature unity – she

allowed too little to any law outside herself. Had
it been possible for her to find in that blazing
Court of fervid and fantastic adoration any spirit
of authority over her, could she have felt the
mastery of power and greatness and, half against,
half with her will, been subordinated to it, she
might have found the thing she chiefly lacked and
obscurely desired – lucid recognition of something mightier than herself. None could give it –
neither Leicester nor Cecil, neither Hatton nor
Walsingham, nor Essex at the end. The greatest
spirits of her reign were separated from her –
Shakespeare by degree and Bacon by age. She
was left to wander in the dark night of existence,
and only in her unfathomed heart to believe
dimly in the motions of a mysterious God.

Meanwhile she continued to drive before the
car of her spectacular Majesty the else irrecon-
cilable minds of her councillors. She enjoyed the
small strain of their dislikes and inamities, knowing they dared not break into hostility, nor impose
on her any but a temporary crisis. She maintained Leicester ; she kept Cecil ; her favours and
her fierce irritations flew variably over them.
Her intelligence, her pride, her royalty, derived
nourishment from the subdued contentions. She
sustained herself and the land was quiet.

But when the trumpets suddenly sounded the
death of Francis, King of France, the prospect
changed a little. Mary Stuart was about to

return to Scotland. She applied (still refusing to
ratify the treaty) to Elizabeth for a safe-conduct,
to allow her, if she chose or was compelled by
storm, to pass through England on her way to
her native kingdom. No one was very anxious
to have her there – not the Lords of the Congregation, nor Elizabeth of England, nor Philip of
Spain. The new French Government was
anxious to have her out of France. Elizabeth
refused to send the safe-conduct unless Mary
ratified the treaty. Mary preferred to remain
Catholic and royal claimant, and in a superb
Renascence style played her part of prospective
victim. If she was compelled to land, she told
Elizabeth's ambassador, " the Queen your mistress will have me in her hands to do her will of
me . . . she may do her pleasure and make
sacrifice of me." She embarked. Elizabeth sent
a safe-conduct too late. It was generally expected,
nevertheless, in France, in Spain, in Scotland,
that Mary would be seized upon the way. She
was left untouched ; she landed.

It was clear with her coming that something
had better be done between the two kingdoms,
and embassies began to pass to determine exactly
what. The Queens, maintaining their technical
division, began to express personal affection.
Mary suggested that she should be recognized as
heir-presumptive ; Elizabeth, that she herself
should first be recognized as reigning Queen.

Elizabeth was uneasily aware that heirs-presump-
tive, with or without their own consent, were
thorns to sovereigns. "Think you," she said to
Mary's ambassador, "that I could love my
winding sheet? . . . I have good experience
of myself in my sister's time, how desirous men
were that I should be in place, and earnest to
set me up. And if I would have consented, I
know what enterprises would have been attempted
to bring it to pass." Proposals for meeting were
made ; the Queens, exchanging presents, ap-
plauded the idea. The Scottish ambassador,
Maitland of Lethington, was urgently in favour.
He thought one of the two women would domi-
nate, but that some arrangement would be made.
He looked farther than any ; he desired more.
"We shoot," he wrote to Cecil, "both at one
scope – the union of this isle." Cecil's almost
permanent sense of disillusion with his mistress
had reached one of its periodical pits of despair ;
he was talking of resignation and the illimitable
ills that would fall on the country under his
successors. The Council took alarm at the
proposed meeting and made speeches. The
Queen, in full session, defied them. She, Mary,
and Maitland pressed on the arrangements. It
was fixed for the end of August or the beginning
of September, somewhere in North England.
It was prevented by another outbreak of war.

The Huguenots in France had been attacked
Ee

by Mary's friends and relatives, the House of
Guise. In France the national mass had swayed
on to the Roman Catholic side, and the Counter-
Reformation threatened to triumph. The civil
war which followed on the first outbreak alarmed
all Protestant feeling in England, and it was this
alarm which had made the Council so strongly
anti-Marian. The Huguenots appealed to the
Queen, and the Queen consented to aid them.
Besides the necessity of checking the Counter-
Reformation, there was a minor theme in the
decision – the hope of Calais. Elizabeth had
failed to recover it by negotiation ; she demanded
it now as a compensation for armed help. The
help was sent, and was of no use. The war
petered out ; Catherine de Medici, who was not
much more metaphysically minded than Elizabeth herself, managed a peace.· The French
unanimously agreed to dislike the English in-
vaders, and the Queen, having suffered military
defeat and diplomatic disaster, was compelled to
withdraw her troops.

The atmosphere was heavier than of old, with
cloudy menace. In 1562 the Queen fell ill of
smallpox ; she recovered, but there had been
intense anxiety. The utterly unforeseen future
emphasized itself. Mary Stuart was in Scotland
and marriageable ; the Guises were in touch with
her and with Philip of Spain ; Philip could con-
template an arrangement with her which did not

add weight to France, and the militant Catholicism of the Guises chimed with his own. The marriage problems of both Queens came to the front. Elizabeth, while always snubbing the Commons that spoke of hers, always encouraged foreign Princes to do so. There was talk of her marrying Charles, King of France ; there was talk of Mary marrying Don Carlos of Spain. There was renewed talk of the succession. Suggestions became schemes, and schemes more and more complex. In the summer of 1564 Elizabeth introduced a new pattern. She made one of those strange emotional moves which utterly defeat the mind of the later reader, a move which would be so wild an insult that it must be regarded as a serious altruism, so romantic that it must have been meant as intelligent. She proposed to Maitland that Mary should marry Lord Robert Dudley.

It was almost universally believed that he and the Queen had been lovers ; it had been a scandal everywhere. When she had thought herself dying she had declared that there had been nothing scandalous between them. In her strength, though she loved gossip, she was careless of scandal. She offered Dudley to Mary as the most intimate sign of her goodwill. It was a fantastic and unbelievable, but an actual and apparently a sincere gesture ; yet the offer had in it an Elizabethan twist. She told Sir James

Melville that she knew, if the marriage took place, Dudley would not allow any attempt to thrust her from the Throne of England. The proposal defeated Maitland ; it at first angered and then perplexed Mary. The same thought struck both of them : did this mean a promise of the succession ? It apparently did not. Elizabeth conceived herself perhaps as offering Mary a gift of more value than many successions ; it was not her own scheme of values, but she probably convinced herself emotionally that it ought to be Mary's. " You think, Madam," Melville told her, " that if you were married you would be but Queen of England, and now you are both King and Queen. I know your spirit cannot endure a commander."

There was, however, another man younger and better born than Dudley, great-grandson of Henry VII through the House of Lennox, and therefore not altogether out of touch with the succession. His name was Henry, Lord Darnley. Mary played with the idea, and, when the Don Carlos match fell through, played with it more ardently. The Lennoxes had fled to England in the reign of Henry VIII, and had been there since. If Mary could not by her marriage unite Roman Catholicism internationally, and put herself in the way of a great empire, by this at least she could draw herself even closer to the Throne of two kingdoms, and draw nearer the Roman Catholic masses in England and Scotland.

She could, in fact, make through the whole island a distinctively Marian and Roman party.

Elizabeth, since the Dudley plan looked like failing, and since she certainly did not wish Mary to contract a menacing foreign marriage, put no serious obstacles in the way. Against the Council's wish she let Darnley go to Scotland. Mary passionately approved him – " the best-proportioned long man she had seen." Elizabeth kept Dudley with her in England ; she made him Earl of Leicester. There were intimacies of touch even at the investiture. Mary became certain that Elizabeth was playing with her ; she created Darnley Earl of Ross. Elizabeth ordered him to return. He did nothing of the kind. Elizabeth sent formal protests against the marriage, which was now definitely proposed. But as between a Continental alliance and a marriage with Dudley, perhaps, when it came to the point, Darnley was the best compromise. She allowed it to happen ; in June 1565 it took place.

Its success was modified by the prompt rebellion of the Scottish Protestant lords. Mary made short work of them and Elizabeth disowned them. She ranted at them in public. But at least the work had been done by Mary's own troops ; no French or Spanish army had entered. There had been no promise of the succession. The Queen of England had once more compromised with events, and had emerged, as the next few years were to show, in a position of increased strength. Darnley's character was such that Mary, it was soon clear, had all the disadvantages and none of the advantages of a political marriage, and all the disadvantages and none of the advantages of a romantic. Elizabeth remained with none of the disadvantages of a romantic marriage and as many of the advantages as her secret relation with Leicester permitted, while being free, at the same time, to contract a political, and (now Mary was maritally out of the way) being again the best match in Europe. The beautiful hands, of which she was so proud, could still be alluringly stretched out to any suitor ; and if the face, now past its early youth, pitted with smallpox, and vitalized by fierce eyes, was not of the first beauty, there lay still above the yellowish-red hair the gleam of the crown.

It was 1565 ; she was thirty-one, and she had reigned for seven years.

CHAPTER IV

THE next few years accordingly were filled in the
South by more marriage negotiations, in the
North by marriage infelicities. In the North
between 1565 and 1568 came the murder of
Rizzio, the rise of Bothwell, the murder of
Darnley, the defeat and imprisonment of Mary,
and at last her flight. In the South were long
discussions and controversies over a proposed
match – this time with the Archduke Charles. It
came very near to success – so near that it seemed
as if only one thing in the end stood in the way :
might the Archduke, if he consented, and if he
consented so far as even to accompany the Queen
to the English churches, have his own private
Mass in his own private chapel ? Even Elizabeth's Ministers, even Cecil, were ready to con-
cede this. Only, after long hesitation, the Queen
refused. She was certainly not more Protestant
than Cecil, and she refused, partly at any rate,
because she was not. She would not tolerate the
existence, in the very centre of royalty, of an

admitted distinction between the two modes of
faith. On the metaphysical side she blurred the
issue, which, in spite of all her efforts, was becoming more, and more angrily, defined. On the
side of events she was clearer : she would not
allow a rallying-point for disaffection. The
religious controversy in England was different
from that in the Netherlands, in France, in
Scotland – almost in all Europe ; and its peculiar
quality helped to leave Elizabeth undenounced
by Rome and to hold in a vague net all but the
most determined Protestants and Papalists. That
quality was, simply, that the controversy had not
been between Churches, but about – even within
– a Church. There had been no violent schism
between the Marian and Elizabethan settlements.
The buildings remained ; most of their ministers
remained ; the celebrations remained. The chief
events, as it were, of historic Christendom went
straight on in an unbroken succession, as did the
succession of bishops. They might or might not
have lost their religious value, but as exterior
events they remained. As desirable events
Elizabeth was determined that not even the
Archduke's private Mass should be allowed
secretly to contradict their sufficiency ; as undesirable events the Pope, soon now, was to
contradict and denounce them and their
Governor.

From 1568 to 1570 or so came a rush of events.

The first was Mary Stuart. She arrived, a
fugitive sovereign, claiming help, reminding
Elizabeth of old promises, demanding justice. She
asked help from the Princess whose legitimacy
she denied and whose Throne she claimed, in
order that she might again occupy that Throne
from which, if she chose, she might the more
easily attempt to seize this other. A Bayard might
have lived up to such conditions ; Elizabeth
merely considered all the possibilities. She did
not want Mary ; she did not like having her ; but
she had her. There were a number of courses
open : (a) to restore her by force of arms, which
would be difficult and dangerous ; (b) to send her
on to France or Spain, which would present either
country with an incarnate claim to England ;
(c) to hand her over to the Scottish lords, which
would mean her death ; (d) to keep her as a
wronged Princess at the Court of England, which
looked like encouraging her own death or removal;
(e) to keep her in England as more or less of a
prisoner, more or less honourably ; (f) to put her
to death after a show of trial and sentence.

It seemed, in view of the feeling at home and in
Scotland, that (a) was impossible. The Queen's
sense of her own self-preservation made her
reluctant to do (b) or (d). Her guild-sense of
Mary as a sovereign Prince made her abhor (c)
and (f). Remained (e). Elizabeth did not much
want (e). She made spasmodic motions towards

any and all of the others. She said things and
wrote things which encouraged everyone to fear
or hope she was about to take an alternative
course, but she never did – or not for seventeen
years. On metaphysical grounds any course
could be defended except this. Events alone
pointed to this, and she took it. She did not – it
is her disgrace and her glory – invent any kind of
metaphysical theory to account for it. She did
not pretend to like it. She merely said that if,
since, and while she was Queen of England, it was
impossible to do anything else. She added that
it was all very sad and all very difficult.

In the intervals of claiming Elizabeth's help for
her own restoration, Mary claimed the help of the
Papalist sovereigns for the deposition of Elizabeth.
She told both Elizabeth and the sovereigns that a
very little help would do. When she was Queen
of England she would restore Catholicism, and if
(she cried out in anger) the Grand Turk would
help her to her rights she would call in the Grand
Turk. She demanded from Elizabeth the most
correct observance of the most exact duty, reserv-
ing to herself the widest limits of possible convenience. If ever a position could be called
" impossible," it was the position of those two
women, yet it lasted for seventeen years. In those
years many wild and hysterical things were said
by both Queens, many foolish and wicked things
done. Through those years the will of Elizabeth,

forced by events yet contending with events,
preserved Mary's life and forbade her freedom,
in a combination of courage and timidity, obstinacy and weakness, honour and falsehood. The
one certain thing is that Elizabeth remained on
the throne and Mary remained alive – in a world
where, a little later, even a high ecclesiastic and
diplomat of the Papal Court declared that the
assassination of a heretic sovereign was an act
well pleasing to God.

Mary, like Elizabeth in her earlier days, took
at one time to the ritual of her custodian ; she
adopted the Book of Common Prayer. But she
also said quite frankly that it was no good her
losing her reputation among the Roman Catholic
champions if she was uncertain of Elizabeth's
friendship. On the whole, what with her trust
in God and her distrust of the Queen of England,
she found the old ways the best. It was as she
settled to this determination that there chanced
three events which determined the formal breach
between Elizabeth and the Roman principles.
They were (i) the Spanish gold, (ii) the Northern
Rebellion, (iii) the Excommunication. They determined that half of the Queen's vision of herself
should dissolve into air.

(i) The affair of the Spanish gold took place in
the year 1568. The King of Spain had been
dealing, through his lieutenant, the Duke of Alva,
with heretical and economic revolts in the

Netherlands. They had been crushed, but the crushing had cost money. Philip borrowed money ; the Italian bankers agreed to let him have a loan. It was agreed that it should be shipped under his care to the Netherlands, and the actual loan should begin upon its arrival there. It seems as if the Italians determined to make the Spanish Government pay the cost of transport, and the Government decided to cut down the cost ; the ships carrying it had practically no convoy. Near England, French and English privateers got on the track; the unhappy Spanish merchantmen fled into English ports. Under the moral pressure and warnings of the English port governors, the Spanish captains unloaded their chests of gold. Posts rode to London. The Queen, stirred, as always, by the idea of a great deal of gold, commanded the treasure to be brought up also.

The Spanish ambassador asked for an audience to demand safe-conduct for the gold. Meanwhile he wrote to Alva desiring that all English goods and ships should be arrested. He meant it as a precautionary measure or a threat ; Alva consented. The Queen's advisers (including a French cardinal) urged Elizabeth to keep the gold ; while she hesitated, it was discovered that it did not yet belong to Philip, but to the bankers. With immediate celerity, the Queen arranged to borrow it herself; the bankers, not being in a position to refuse, consented. But when she heard of the arrest of her ships and goods, so unwisely arranged before her decision was taken, she broke into rage. A similar arrest was immediately put on all Flemish and Spanish goods in England, and the result was heavily in favour of the English. The Queen had the goods and the money too. The infinite patience of the King of Spain endured. But the already strained relations which had been established when, nine years before, in answer to his stupendous offer of himself, Elizabeth had promised to be a sister to him ("sister and perpetual confederate") received yet more exacerbation. Some years later, it is only just to add, the money was returned to him.

The effect on the Netherlands was disastrous. Alva was deprived of his money, and trade was damaged. To pay his troops, Alva put a tax on all sales, and damaged trade still more heavily. Prices soared; competition with other countries suffered. Shops were closed in protest. Orthodox Catholics regarded the Catholic Spanish army with new and hostile eyes. A revolt which had been mostly religious and sporadic became economic and universal. Catholic governors were expelled, fighting Calvinists welcomed. Philosophical toleration among the rebels became a necessity, and the Spanish army therefore found itself with a great deal to do.

(ii) Elizabeth had had, on the whole, a quiet country, but the northern half of it was only partly hers. There, between the mass of her subjects and the influence of the Throne, lay the more immediate territorial power of the great Northern lords, the Percys and the Dacres. There the Roman tradition was strongest, in spite of the operation of the bishops ; and from the North the greatest possibility of revolt had threatened.

The arrival of Mary in England sent a thrill through all the quiescent opposition to the Government. Elizabeth was surrounded by the power of the Families, but even among the Families there were divisions. The older group – the Families in being – leaned to territorialism and the Catholic tradition ; the newer – the Families who were only becoming – to centralization and the Protestant doctrine. The Queen swayed equal in the midst – knowing them all not as names and abstractions but as persons. In the end the Marian attraction was a misfortune for the older group. Between sympathy for Mary and support for Mary was not a wide margin ; between support for Mary and sedition to the Queen, less ; between sedition and full treason, even less. Mary's fatal claim to the Throne, potential always, if un-mentioned, ensured that.

The Families stirred, as it were, in their sleep. Dim hints, vague menaces, began to pass. It was suggested that the Duke of Norfolk, the Queen's noblest and richest subject, would be a fit match for Mary Stuart. He was a Protestant noble of thirty-three (he had had Foxe of the *Book of Martyrs* as a tutor), but his position was high, next to the Blood, and he had shown feeling for Mary, over the inquiry into whose statements, held in 1568, he had presided. It was proposed to marry him to Mary, to restore her to Scotland (on the condition of a general indemnity to her enemies), to establish her in the succession, and to cause a palace revolution in England, overthrowing Cecil. Leicester was in the secret; so was Cecil, though that was in spite of the confederates.

The marriage had first been proposed in the previous year; then the Queen had challenged Norfolk on it. In answer he had protested that, since Mary pretended a title, " your Majesty," if this were true, " might justly charge me with seeking your own crown from your head." If this was how it struck Norfolk, it had certainly struck Elizabeth in the same way. But she was willing to restore Mary, and – on terms – she might have put up with the marriage, watching to see what success the Protestant Howard and the Roman Stuart made of it (Mary had been three times married before this; so had the Duke). She spoke lightly to him once, after he had dined with her; she twitched his ear, and bade him

" take heed of his pillow." He remained obstin-
ately silent; she spoke of it on a later day, saying
she wished to hear the truth from himself. He
admitted something; she commanded him to go
no farther in that matter.

But this was not so easy, and the final purposes
of all the confederates were not so limited as
Norfolk's own. There was to be a rising in the
North; Alva in the Netherlands was to be asked
for support; the Spanish ambassador was con-
sulted by everyone. Mary had written tender
letters to the Duke, but the tenderness was
tendentious – to the stuffed velvet of a double
crown. No harm was said to be intended to
Elizabeth. But she was at the least to be told
firmly what she must do. Cecil had faded away
from the confederation; Leicester began to back
out. The Queen sent for Norfolk; he said he
was ill and fled into the country, sending messages
to beg the Northern earls not to move. The ports
were closed; the angry Mary was carried to
another residence, the Duke peremptorily ordered
to return. He did not dare refuse; he feared
too greatly the fierce temper of Elizabeth. First
he again pleaded illness, then he came.

It was herself, and her energy, and Cecil,
against a very heavy mass. She was intensely
angry; her vision of herself as the loving mother
of her people was outraged, and she was wild to
restore it. She threw Norfolk into the Tower,

and summoned the Earls of Northumberland and Westmorland to London. Their men rose even before they had decided, before they wanted, to lead them. The army marched; in Durham they tore up the English service books and heard the Latin Mass. They hovered down, past York, and back again. They took Hartlepool, to give them a harbour for Alva's troops. Alva sent none. The Queen's levies, from all the rest of the kingdom, came pressing north. There was no compensating outbreak anywhere else. Disheartened, the rebellion did not meet the Queen's troops. They fled, and carnage followed them. Elizabeth struck at every village which favoured revolt. The Earls had escaped, but the poor could not escape. It was – for Elizabeth and England – a dreadful vengeance, though perhaps, for that age and that Europe, it was not so out of the way. It was final; in the days of the Armada there was no rebellion. The Queen had saved her State; it was certainly her State and not a complete England she had saved. It was above all a salvation dictated in her mind by no particular scheme of theology; what she avenged was not a doctrine but herself. She had no greater virtue and at that time no greater sin.

(iii) Doctrine, however, would not rest quiet; it is not in its nature. By 1569 the hopes of the Counter-Reformation that Elizabeth might be converted were failing, and even the hope that

F E

she might be vicariously converted by marriage to a husband in communion with Rome. To the devout and distant foreigner, unless he moved in the highest circles of Spanish or French diplomacy, she began to seem a curiously fabulous and archetypal heretic, and indeed they were right. From almost any doctrinal point of view, she was something of a heretic. " I see many overbold with God Almighty, making too subtle scannings of his blessed will," she said once. She had been, in the shaping years of her youth, too much sworn sister to " grim Necessity," and her sisterhood was touched with irony. The mere language of the extreme doctrinalists offended her, and the habit of their minds. But to them in turn she began to grow gigantic, monstrous, and unnatural, putting forth many arms. She who was to have been nowhere began to be everywhere ; she who might have been given the crown as a gift obtruded it as a right. Her power and her influence wandered subtly through the Christian world, nor had it yet pleased God to remove her. Mary Stuart was in her prison, and her feet were crimson with the blood of the faithful. In the centre of Roman Christendom the Papacy roused itself to strike at the bastard heretic who had already sat for twelve years on her Throne, the most ostentatious defiance of the recovery of Christendom. Paul IV and Pius IV had spared her, helped thereto by the continual expression

of the wishes of Philip of Spain. Pius V spared
her for five years. But the time for that for-
bearance which has been often, not unjustly,
claimed as a quality of the Roman See,
had gone by. There had been some kind of
intention of smiting at her with the spiritual
sword while the Northern Earls struck with the
temporal ; unfortunately for the alliance, the
swords were drawn at different moments, and the
temporal was already broken. But the spiritual
was dangerous enough. In February 1570 the
Pope issued the Bull *Regnans in Excelsis*. Elizabeth
was declared illegitimate, excommunicate, dia-
bolical, " a servant of all iniquity." Her subjects
were freed from their allegiance ; her laws were
declared void ; her person was terribly outcast
from civilization and mankind in this world, and
her soul from salvation and redeemed mankind
in the next. In awful and perilous words she
was " severed from the body of Christ." In May
the Bull was fixed by a devoted servant of the
Roman See, a young student of Lincoln's Inn,
by name John Felton, to the door of the Bishop
of London's house in St. Paul's Churchyard.
Anathema was immediately answered by execution ; the tortured body of Felton exhibited the
defiance of the Queen.

The Bull exhorted the Catholic sovereigns to
act. They left it to Felton. The Emperor and
the King of Spain wrote, almost rebuking their

spiritual lord. Philip especially was very stiff with him. The King of France refused to allow the publication of the Bull in his dominions, and, as it were, pretended it had not happened. This was not wholly altruism ; it was not to the interest of sovereign orthodox States that doctrine should depose kings, even heretical kings. Heresy was a chameleon-like word. But in spite of their anger, the thing was done. The whole population in England were officially commanded to be martyrs or victors ; any who refused were, *ipso facto*, sharers in the sin and the doom. Elizabeth, who had been slowly living down her illegitimacy, was confronted with a fervent declaration of it as *regnans in excelsis*. She was placarded to Europe as in fact no Queen. She was thrown violently on to the side of Cecil and his new assistant, the Puritan Francis Walsingham. From that day she regarded – and rightly regarded – every missionary priest who landed in England as an enemy to her person and her Throne, formally in doctrine, potentially in practice.

In 1570, therefore, in her own view she was at unspoken odds with Spain ; she had been outraged by her people, and outraged by Rome. It was the decision of the permanent breach. She was thirty-seven, and the perfection of her desire had been dissipated,

CHAPTER V

BEHIND all the shows, the pageants, of London, and the long splendours of the progresses ; behind the dances, the masques, the dicing, and the hunting ; behind the diplomacies, and the amours, and the religions ; behind the cultures – the Roman Catholic, the Protestant, and that third style of mind which may be called Shakespearean, because, though Shakespeare was yet only a boy of six at Stratford, the matter which he was to vivify with his genius was already in being, and a mode of consciousness was being prepared for its education under his mature power, so that the intellectual heart of England would never be the same again – behind all these things, in some of which the Queen took her delight and of some of which she was as profoundly ignorant as Cecil, there lay in her mind the steady matter of money. She had come to a throne impoverished by blackmail, by robbery, and by devotion ; she set to work to restore it. Implicitly, and without a full consciousness of the purpose of her labour, she toiled to forestall the domination of the Families. They throve under her as under her predecessors ; their estates grew. She massed her Treasury in their midst ; it was for this that, with them, she took so vivid an interest in the voyages to the ends of the world. She took pleasure in the daring of her captains, and rejoiced in their romanticism, but for her, as for all the capitalists who encouraged them, it was gold and other precious commodities which were the great purpose. Among the commodities were negro slaves. In the year 1564 the Earl of Pembroke, the Lord Admiral, and the Lord Robert Dudley had shares, and Cecil took a close interest, in a slaving voyage arranged by John Hawkins, who gathered four hundred slaves on the coast of Africa and disposed of them to the Spanish colonists of the West Indies and South America, not without some threat of force. The Queen lent him a ship of the Royal Navy, the *Jesus of Lübeck*. The *Jesus*, it is proper to note, was severely strained by the voyage. Hawkins had to pay for its repair. The profit on the expedition – on the goods brought back from the West rather than directly on the slaves, but the slaves paid for the goods – was said by the Spanish ambassador to be 60 per cent. The slave-trade had been discouraged by the Spanish Government, and one of the officials who traded with Hawkins was punished. Cecil and Leicester recommended the Queen to grant Hawkins a coat of arms, which she did : " sable, on a point wavy a lion passant or ; in chief three bezants ; for a crest, a demi-Moor proper bound in a cord."

As for gold, in 1577 there was a voyage to Baffin Land where it was thought to have been discovered. The Queen, Leicester, Cecil, Walsingham, Philip Sidney, all had shares. It was unfortunate ; the ore brought back yielded no gold, and the capitalists lost their money. Negro slaves were safer.

It may be said for Elizabeth that her gains, when they existed, went into the necessities of government – to the upkeep of the Navy, for example, for which she was expected to pay. Her usual method was to lend ships and take a proportion of the whole profits of the expedition.

It was not only by sea that the policies of the Queen, especially since the Excommunication, distracted the action of Spain ; they crept also through the Flanders lands recovered from the sea, amphibious Protestant beasts which the Papal decree had now defined and denounced as of the tribe of hell. Hell is a game at which two can play ; unlike heaven, which is a game played peculiarly by its single self. Antichrist was a name of many applications ; it could be used for the Pope as easily as the Queen, and more and more the Queen's servants applied it to him. The Queen, having failed to combine

the two contending metaphysics in the event of
her remarkable person, was compelled to lean
in diplomacy towards one of them. She never
identified herself with it. Walsingham's godli-
ness and Cecil's precisianism were not for her.
But she was compelled to support them in action,
though she might hate them in theory, and they
had no doubts of their duty. Away in the West,
among " evening isles fantastical," the English
pirates crept, small fortresses of hostility ; narrow
rivulets of hostility – English money, English
credit, English volunteers, English secret com-
missions – flowed tortuously through the Netherlands. On the other side, the heat of the fires
that burned or the rattle of the chains that bound
an occasional English sailor who had offended
the dogmas of the Papacy or the dominion of
Spain were blown across the seas. Both sides
were fretted ; they were not maddened. Events
dragged both Philip and Elizabeth on ; so far
as they could, they dragged events back.

In 1571 the Parliament declared it to be high
treason to call the Queen a heretic – the Act was
an epigram of articulation, unsound in its ter-
minology. " England entered upon a course of
persecution " – formally. Its distinguishing mark
was that it was persecution not merely in defence
of the State – that all persecution had always
been ; the Calvinists whom Mary Tudor or Alva
destroyed were destroyed as rebels as much as

the Jesuits who perished at Tyburn. It was persecution in defence of a State which culminated in a Princess who was the expression rather of a series of events than a philosophical theory, who was in fact solely a person. The Church she governed (in some views) was helped, by the introduction into its history of this series of events, to recover a quality – freedom, tolerance, comprehensiveness, whatever it is called – which made it not less after the mind of Christ than any other. Certainly no theory which allows that the action of Kings may affect without invalidating the election of a Pope can deny, except by dogma, that the actions of a Queen may have similarly restored grace to the Church.

In 1571 the third of the blows which shaped the Queen's habit of mind for the remainder of her reign took place. The Northern Rebellion had disturbed and alarmed her ; the Excommunication had angered her ; this other thing was more secret and, at its end, felt as more intimate, than those public attacks. It is known as the Ridolfi plot. Ridolfi was one of the more important Italians in London, a Roman Catholic, a banker, a man of high social standing and of easily hopeful temperament. He was in contact with the Spanish ambassador, as everyone always was, from Mary Stuart to Sir John Hawkins. He was also in contact with the Duke of Norfolk, who had been released from the Tower at Cecil's motion after making complete submission and promising fidelity. Ridolfi made himself the focus of a new plot. The idea of marrying Norfolk to Mary was renewed ; aid was to be procured from Spain - arms, money, and men. The aims were as before - the restoration of Mary to her Throne and of the Roman obedience throughout the island. Ridolfi left England (after an interview with the Queen on the previous Sunday) and went to Alva.   Alva refused to send aid until the insurrection was in being ; if, he thought, the revolting English could defy the Queen for about six weeks, then the enterprise would be worth supporting. Ridolfi passed on to Rome, secured support, and came at last to Madrid.   Somewhere on the way the assassination of Elizabeth was added to the plan, as a final touch of polish.   It was discussed by the King of Spain's Council.

The spies maintained systematically by the English Government followed up the plot in the Low Countries and in England. By them, and by chance aiding them, the details came to Cecil (created in 1571 Lord Burghley). The exposure of the conspiracy led to a violent burst of public horror and excitement, and to a concentrated agitation against Mary. Elizabeth herself was shaken ; a new thing had intimately entered her life - the possibility of sudden and secret death. Vaguely it might have been imagined earlier,

but now it had come to words. In the high places
of Europe her taking-off had, she heard, been a
matter of open discussion. It was true that
Norfolk and Mary were not concerned in this
elaboration of detail. They were quite enough
concerned. Norfolk was again sent to the Tower.
The Spanish ambassador, after a scene with the
Council, was ordered to leave the country, which,
after lingering a little on the chance that Cecil
might be shot by two men detached for the
attempt, he did. The French ambassador, who
spoke for Mary, was answered by the Queen
" in a most furious rage." She fell into a new
mood against Mary, and seemed to have abandoned any possible intention of restoring her.
On 16 January Norfolk was brought to trial and
condemned. Then, suddenly, Elizabeth hesitated. Her nature revolted. He was her ac-
quaintance and her kinsman. Twice she signed,
twice she countermanded the warrant. She did
not certainly feel it as a sin, as she certainly felt
the later execution of Mary as a sin, but she did
not wish to strike one so near herself and to renew
the bloody decrees of old reigns. The weeks slid
by. On 9 April she signed a third warrant ;
at two in the morning of 11 April Cecil was
awakened by a note saying she could not do it :

" My Lord me thinkes that I am more
beholdinge to the hindar part of my hed than

wel dare trust the forwards side of the same, & therefore sent to the Levetenant & the S., as you knowe best, the Ordar to defar this execution till the[y] here furdar. And that this may be done I doubte nothing, without curiositie of my further warrant, for that ther rasche determination upon a very unfit day was countermanded by your considerat admonition. The causes that move me to this ar not now to be expressed, lest an irrevocable dede be in mene while committed. If the[y] wyl nides a Warrant, let this suffice, all written with my none hand.

"Your most lovinge Soveraine."

The whole of the Court, all the vocal part of the country, expected the Duke's execution ; abroad, it was thought more than possible that Mary would also die. For five months the Queen maintained an effort to spare her own subject. It is not perhaps unrelated to her failure that during those months she became involved in an acrimonious correspondence with Mary, both great ladies unsheathing their verbal claws. They both had claws enough, sharpened on facts. Parliament, coming together in May, in speech after speech after speech railed against Mary, presenting ways of dealing with her. The Queen, half yielding, half eluding, at last concluded. She gave way to the pressure ; she consented to

Norfolk's execution ; she consented to nothing more. All proposals against Mary she vetoed with, " La reyne s'avisera." On 2 June he was put to death. Elizabeth was unhappy. The process of things was beginning to put an iron chain on her will, nor could she free herself.

The English were becoming, if not exactly Protestant, then at least non-Roman, except for those Romans who were, by their devotion and their doom, to become even more Roman. They were becoming more patriotic. They were also becoming more vocal. The national mass, deflected to follow her, became with every year more national. It was, so far, her success. Her feminine mind had imposed half of her natural will upon events ; the stamp of the rest was thwarted by supernatural belief. She was a personally popular figure, yet she might be assassinated at any moment. She enjoyed her people ; she enjoyed the sensation of their enjoyment of her. Jests and speeches answered laughter and cheers. She belonged to that small group of princes who – not only in theory but in appearance and behaviour – are at once monarch and person. In the Court she was the centre of Euphuistic delights, and pleasures other than Euphuistic ; in the city she was the patroness of extending trade and stabilized credit ; in the country she was a mistress, if not of curds and whey, at least of cows and cowmen. There were

dark patches enough ; the unemployed, in spite
of the justices, wandered through the country and
hung about the city.   In 1581 the Queen's coach
itself, when she went to take the air, was surrounded at Islington by " a number of rogues,"
which provoked the Recorder of London to a
great clearance ; he swept up something like
250, of whom he remarked with pleasure that not
more than a dozen belonged to London, Middle-
sex, and Surrey.   It is likely that the incident
provoked one of those rages into which she so
often broke.   She threw her shoe at Walsingham ;
she boxed her maids' ears ; she cursed and swore
in a deep contralto at her Ministers and her
menials alike.   She could be rough with preachers
and bishops.   Yet also she was capable of tender-
nesses and generosities.   She could throw a man
into prison and then write to his wife to ease her
fears.   She was capable (on a famous occasion)
of raging at the Polish ambassador in a speech of
furious impromptu Latin.   She was capable of
writing little private notes of sympathy and good
fellowship to her generals and ambassadors, such
as this postscript (of 1562) shows :

> " My deare Warwik if your honor & my
> desir could accord with the los of the nidefuls
> fingar I kipe, God helpe me so in my most
> nide as I wold gladly lis that one joint for your
> safe abode with me, but sins I can not that

I wold, I wil do that I may, & wil rather
drinke in an asin [ashen] cup than you or yours
shude not be soccerd both by sea & land yea &
that with all spede possible, & let this my
scribling hand witness it to them all

                    " Yours as my own E. R."

Behind her the mass, deflected to nationality,
moved. By 1570, those who had been children
at her accession were young men and women ;
babies were children who knew of the Queen,
and had in many cases seen the Queen
when she rode into a provincial city or the train
of coaches of her progress swung slowly down the
winding country roads. She loved the mass, but
sometimes it oppressed her, in nothing more than
in the unresolved matter of Mary Stuart. The
North was quiet ; she had shed blood enough to
ensure that. The South, and the gentlemen who
came to the Parliament, had all the rhetorical
hostility and the easy solutions of the irresponsible.
It was impossible that the Queen should not desire
her rival's death ; she laboured with the wish
and against it. She could not and would not act,
but she could not prevent herself wishing that
something might happen. Similar emotions often
ran riot in the Courts of Paris and Madrid and
Rome concerning herself ; indeed, the high
historic ostentation of royal drama has concealed
from us its universality. It is given to few men

and women to pass through the world without
desiring – even passionately – the death of another,
could it be brought about by some action other
than their own. We are all kindred to the Queen
in that thing ; she only had a chance of action.
Abroad, it was continually expected that she
would act ; the King of France said he knew
what he would do if he were in Elizabeth's
place and had Mary Stuart a prisoner. At home,
it was lamented that she did not act. Once –
in the shock of hearing of the St. Bartholomew –
she was brought to offer to yield Mary to the
Scottish lords if they would certainly put her to
death ; they refused, unless an English force
assisted, and this Elizabeth in turn refused. She
might have meant it ; at the last moment it is
possible, but doubtful, if she would have carried
out the plan. Meanwhile the royal coach swayed
on, and the high, pale face of the Queen smiled
out on her fields, and the beautiful hands gesticu-
lated. Or in the Presence the eyes flashed and
the voice screamed at some folly ; or in the
council chamber the inscrutable gaze passed over
the kneeling lords and delayed on Dudley with
still vivid affection, or lingered with a fantastic
coyness on one of the newer Favourites, or returned again to measure meditative looks with
Cecil, while she listened and acknowledged and
all but, and hardly ever quite, acceded, and he,
bowing, went away, and she rose and went about

her work, and changed from one of her innumerable dresses to another, and adorned herself with jewels, and grew older, and older, and longed to break the lonely secrecy of her will, and again never quite would. Under the domination of that will her young and handsome servants rose one after the other, and clung round her – parasitical brilliance, growing duller with time. Hatton rose – Captain of the Guard in 1572, and Chancellor in 1587, after Raleigh had succeeded to his place as Captain in 1586 ; 1587 also saw the more dangerous creature of the Queen, Essex, already Master of the Horse. She watched their quarrels as she watched the disputes of her Ministers, and with none of them her heart or her policy lay. It is a tenable belief that she was asked by God for one thing alone – surrender ; and that she refused. If so, the thing was made as difficult as possible for her – she was asked to thwart, to contradict, almost to outrage, her whole nature, mental and physical. She was asked for heroic sanctity, and those who represented that demand to her had been Mary her sister, with whom she was in such disharmony, and the Lord Cardinal Pole, and the foreign face of Spain, and the foreign voice of the Pope. She refused ; they may blame her who will.

In foreign affairs the questionable centre lay in the Netherlands. Elizabeth did not want Spanish
Ge

armies there, as little did she desire French. She
did not much care for the Calvinistic dialect of
the Netherlands, either there or in her own
Francis Walsingham at home. She did not speak
it, nor did the Church over whose organization
she presided ; but, as the Duke of Alva once
remarked, convenience must determine the keep-
ing of treaties even among Christian sovereigns.
All the Governments of Europe were engaged,
somewhere, in the game of supporting foreign
minorities against the national Government ;
it was then as much to their metaphysical honour
as it would be considered to their national dishonour now. Events had put the Queen outside
the culture of Roman Catholic Europe, but they
pressed her within the urgent necessities of that
culture, and, since assassination did not touch
her, talk of marriage revived. The most pro-
tracted marriage negotiations in the history of
England opened in 1570 ; they lasted, on and off,
till 1583. Elizabeth was thirty-seven when they
began, and almost fifty when they at last fell
away – and quite fifty when her wooer, or her
wooed, died and she wept for him. He was the
brother of the King of France, first called the
Duke of Anjou, afterwards the Duke of Alençon.

In fact, the person of the proposed husband
changed after the first exchanges ; but both the
first and second were sons of Queen Catherine,
brothers to the King of France, and both, at

different times, bore the title of the Duke of Anjou. The twisted complexity of this detail is an example of all ; and in all the details only two permanent facts exist–that Elizabeth continuously talked of marriage, and that she did not marry. The single fact that might help to illumine us – Elizabeth's capacity to bear children – is still hidden, and historians of the highest eminence hold opposite views on that single fact.[1] Deprived of that knowledge, one is left to observe the Queen talking. It is certain that she liked talking ; it is equally certain that she liked talking about her marriage, though she disliked being voted or petitioned into it by the Houses. She liked it and she found it useful. Wooers – even Roman Catholic wooers – who might be thinking of marriage with Mary Stuart found themselves unconsciously and newly magnetized towards another Throne whence Elizabeth's beautiful regal hand waved to them. In 1570 the hand was raised, ever so coyly, in the direction of the Duke of Anjou, brother of Charles of France. Brothers of the King of France were often troublesome to the King, and both he and Catherine de Medici urged the idea on his brother. But Anjou was a Guise man ; he demanded the private

[1] " Elizabeth knew that no heir could be born of her " (A. W. Pollard, *Political History of England,* 1547-1603, p. 326). " Gossip often tried to explain [her failure to marry] by surmising that Elizabeth was incapable of bearing children. . . . The tongue is an unruly member " (J. E. Neale, *Queen Elizabeth,* p. 220).

Mass in his private chapel. Even the Puritan
Walsingham urged the Queen to consent ; she
declined. The French found themselves signing a
treaty favourable to her, and the marriage faded,
and reappeared presently with another face,
that of the Duke of Alençon, Anjou's younger
brother.

Between the two courtships came that political
operation in the disguise of a theological quarrel
which we call the Massacre of St. Bartholomew.
The disguise was sufficiently realistic to enrage
all the Protestants and delight many of the
Catholics throughout Europe. The provocation
given by the Huguenots was forgotten or approved
by their friends, and the Majesty of England,
whose hangmen had but recently returned from
the executions in the North, put on mourning to
receive the French ambassador. It is a mark of
the difference between things abroad and things
at home.

> *Only people like Us is We,*
> *And everyone else is They.*

But, just in proportion as Catherine seemed
rashly to have given herself over to the Catholic
cause, it became undesirable for Elizabeth by
hostility to provoke her into any greater dependence on the Catholic Guises ; and in the same
proportion that the rashness seemed to have
thrown Catherine on to the Spanish side, it

became desirable for Catherine herself to recover ground. The diplomatic manœuvres and conversations, interrupted by that dreadful midnight tocsin of Paris, began again. A full account of a single month of their complications would fill too many books of this size. In the first movements there was a closer connexion between Elizabeth and Philip ; then, as a weight in their scale, the French Government cast the person of the Duke of Alençon. He was eighteen when serious discussions began, without any such scruples as his brother had shown, not handsome, pock-marked, and eager to do something or other – especially, once the chance was his, to marry Elizabeth, even if she were (as she was) forty. He was especially anxious to do something in the Low Countries, and Elizabeth was anxious that he should, so long as he did no more than she wanted, and did not seize them for France.

The whole affair divides into two parts ; the first diplomatic, lasting till 1576, the second personal, beginning in 1578. Its interest here is chiefly in the fact that during the second period the Queen was driven nearer than ever before to a pretence of doing what she had been pretending a readiness to do. Alençon took charge of the affair himself, and, poor creature that he might look, he took the right way with the Queen. He supplied, at a moment when her very high intelligence told her that the adorations of her

English minions were taking on yearly more of flattery and less of exactitude, a new, different, and ardent enthusiasm. The Queen had never before had marriage urged upon her by quite so close a possibility, and never had any possibility urged it more thrillingly. At the beginning of 1579 came Alençon's servant, Jean de Simier, who began making love on his master's account with an enthusiasm which made it seem his own. He had perfectly the measure of Elizabeth's amorous technique ; he played it with all skill. "This discourse," said the French ambassador, "rejuvenates the Queen." Alençon himself came over in August, and took up the siege. The Queen melted, reciprocated, flattered, sighed, flirted madly. The Duke departed, but Simier lingered, and the Queen lingered with Simier.

Agitation rose in the country and the City. The pulpit denounced ; Elizabeth went angrily out in the middle of a sermon. A book was issued ; Elizabeth had the right hands of author and publisher struck off. She was very angry ; whether she could or would marry, no one but she knew, and perhaps not she. It was intolerable to her that she should be bullied. The Council met and argued. Cecil was strongly in favour ; Leicester was against. They determined to ask her what her own wish was ; then they would offer their opinion. At this she grew into worse anger. She told them furiously she had expected to have been desired to marry and have a child of her body. But no anger could persuade them to come to any conclusion except upon her instructions. It was what she did not want to give. To marry Alençon would be to lose herself and her kingdom in appendages, marital and political, of the probable future King of France. To refuse would be to throw away her last chance of marriage, and (what perhaps counted as much) of talking about it. It is no small loss when a vivid cerebralist comes to an age when his mental activity can no longer have any relation to actuality, and to be deprived of a fantasy is as painful as to be deprived of a fact. She clung, diplomatically and personally, to the two terms in the phrase " French marriage," clung the more irritably that Simier had revealed to her the year-old secret marriage of Leicester – Leicester, who had been arguing against her own. Leicester was flung from Court ; Walsingham was in retirement ; Philip Sidney, his son-in-law, who had written to her rhetorically against the marriage, was in disgrace. But Simier also left for France in November. Articles had been signed. She had insisted in them on being given two months to reconcile her people.

The negotiations, the two months being up, floated on. Elizabeth talked about religion ; Alençon talked about money. Elizabeth and Catherine attempted to manipulate each other

into war with Spain, and, each defeating the
other, remained still ostensibly at peace. Ostensibly at peace meant continuous ostentations of
unofficial war. The Jesuit missionaries had
landed in England. They were strictly forbidden
to have anything to do with politics. But they
were regarded as an Order peculiarly Papal ;
and the Bull of Excommunication was also
peculiarly Papal. The chief foreign Roman
Catholic Government regarded them with ap-
proval. " Those who have recently come hither,"
wrote the Spanish ambassador to Philip, " pray
continually for Your Majesty, recognizing that
God has been pleased to make you His principal
instrument in this great work." The English Government felt precisely that Philip was extremely
likely to be the principal instrument in the work.

English Roman Catholics had been dispensed
from rebellion until there was some hope of success. The Government did not propose to permit
them any hope of success from within. But the
energy of those holy souls who gave themselves
to the " Enterprise of England " was immediately
rewarded. A cheerful devotion, a readiness for
loss and even martyrdom, awoke in the Papalist
remnant of England. The lapsed were won, new
converts made, faith and hope increased and
nourished. All the signs of a great revival went
abroad.

In 1580 Philip of Spain put William of Orange

under the ban, declaring him " out of law," with
a price on his head. The Queen of England
heard of it ; she knew of the correspondence of
Mary of Scots ; she did not know at what moment
the dispensation of quiescence given to her
Roman subjects might be withdrawn, nor what
possibilities of murder hovered round her every
day.   She consented to a thing against her temper
and her will, but not (in her view) sinful, any more
than Norfolk's execution – the closer execution of
the penal laws. She limited them as far as
possible ; her Ministers complained that she
would not believe in the danger. But still she
consented to the disunion of the English ; and it
had been the union of the English which, outside
her passing excitements and her personal delights,
she had chiefly in her heart desired. So far, she
was defeated by Cecil and the Pope. In effect,
however, she had been defeated long before – at
the moment of her birth. The conditions of her
birth defeated her desires, and the mother by
whom she had been born to the Throne refused
her the unbloody and wholly popular Throne of
her dreams. The sign of it was the execution,
that year, of Edmund Campion.

It was in 1580, as if in compensation, that
Drake returned from his voyage round the world,
with much Spanish treasure seized in the West.
Elizabeth went down to Deptford, taking the
French ambassador with her, approved him,

jested with him, and caused the ambassador to knight him. It was almost a demonstration of unity between the two countries. Creeds had receded very far into the background in international affairs, however catastrophic they might still be in national. The Queen and the ambassador returned together to London.

The next year saw a sudden revival of the marriage idea, and Alençon once more in London. It was on this visit that the Queen sent a private note to Cecil, telling him of the arrival, and adding, " Let me know what you wish me to do." It is impossible to believe that Cecil planned the lengths to which the Queen was said to have gone; but it is unlikely that she wrote so in regard to a Prince with whom she was passionately in love. Yet as the days ran by she encouraged and shared the love-making, as if in a kind of abandonment of herself. On 22 November, 1581, she went farther than she had ever gone in her personal commitment. The Spanish ambassador wrote to Philip : " I wrote . . . on the 20th, and on the following day Alençon and all his company displayed, not discontent alone, but entire disillusion as to the marriage taking place. On the 22nd, however, at eleven in the morning, the Queen and Alençon were walking together in a gallery, Leicester and Walsingham being present, when the French ambassador entered and said that he wished to write to his master, from whom he had received orders to hear from the Queen's own lips her intention with regard to marrying his brother. She replied, ' You may write this to the King : that the Duke of Alençon shall be my husband,' and at the same moment she turned to Alençon and kissed him on the mouth, drawing a ring from her own hand and giving it to him as a pledge. Alençon gave her a ring of his in return, and shortly afterwards the Queen summoned the ladies and gentlemen from the presence chamber in the gallery, repeating to them in a loud voice in Alençon's presence what she had previously said."

But a month later she told the Earl of Sussex that " she hated the idea of marriage every day more," and devoted herself energetically to getting rid of Alençon. She agreed to lend him sixty thousand pounds (he had already had thirty thousand) ; and on the last day of the year she paid him ten thousand.

Recourse was had to the most extreme measures ; it is said his personal servants were bribed to persuade him to go. Elizabeth's demands on the King of France shot up. On 1 February, 1582, he went, but before he finally embarked he asked for the other fifty thousand. He did not get it. The Queen, who had accompanied him as far as Canterbury, returned to London and the indulgence of her safer emotions. She wept ; she sighed for Alençon ; she was angry with

Leicester, who had been rude about him, and with Walsingham ; and from a safe distance she went on talking about marriage.   But it all came to nothing ; Alençon's fiery shaft was quenched. Presently he died.

CHAPTER VI

Ignorance of Mary Stuart – Walsingham – the Babington plot –
  Elizabeth's dilemma – she consents to sin – opinion in
  Europe – the Spanish "Enterprise of England" – the last of
  the Crusades – defeat of the Armada – death of Leicester.

THE events of the years 1569–70 had determined
the Queen's position ; the events of 1580 had
confirmed it. The events of 1585–8 determined
her success in that position. Mary Stuart, a
royal prisoner still, was ignorant of the slow
change. The years betrayed her ; she thought
still that a little help might be found and would
be sufficient. Time stood still with her ; she
thought that elsewhere things stood still in time.
It was not so ; to name only the greatest change –
James VI sat on the Scottish throne, and, while
she still plotted to gain the English kingdom, she
had in effect lost her own. It seems now to be
rather James than Elizabeth whose intangible
influence kept her in custody ; her great rival was
half inclined to release her with certain formal
conditions. Only the romanticism of Mary's
story still went about, and her religion supported
it. If her adherents could be gathered, encouraged, vivified, she might still have a chance in
England ; in Scotland, except from England, she
had little more. When she had flung the blazon

of the English royal arms abroad in Paris eighteen
years before, Elizabeth had been in a desperate
position ; now the position was reversed. Mary
had but one chance, and her enemies knew it
even if she did not realize it. The game was no
longer between claims and crowns but between
lives ; her single possibility was the death of the
Queen. If a dagger found Elizabeth's heart, a
crown – two crowns – might still rest on Mary's
head. If, that is, Philip of Spain did not prefer
to take it for himself or his family ; in the general
clarification this was thought of ; the King, it
was remarked, was descended from the old House
of Lancaster. There was some difference between the Pope and Philip on who should dispose
of the English egg. As it happened, the egg was
never laid.

It was Mary's first misfortune that this narrow-
ing of the issue was not apparent to her, and that
she was still engaged in as many conspiracies as
ever. Even the Bond of Association, created by
Cecil and the Council in 1584, did not check her ;
though by it, in the event of an attempt on
Elizabeth's life, all the signatories – and it was
very widely signed – pledged themselves to pursue
to the death the person for whose profit the deed
was done. At the same time many of the
signatories, in case the deed succeeded, privately
made efforts to keep on good terms with Mary.
Her second misfortune was the nature of the man

who was now Secretary of State – Francis Walsingham. He was as much a child of Puritan
ideas as she of Catholic, and he came more near
in his heart to regarding her as a daughter of
Satan than probably the Pope to thinking
Elizabeth a child of hell. He hated, as he saw it,
the thing for which she stood, and he was as
unscrupulous as she in fighting for his cause.
Elizabeth no more liked him than Queen Victoria
liked Mr. Gladstone, though Victoria did not
throw shoes. Walsingham insisted on regarding
her as an ally in the service of God ; the Queen
was not apt to think she certainly knew God's
will ; and she thought she was God enough for
Walsingham. Mary's third and culminating misfortune was the fact that Elizabeth was capable
of sin.

Walsingham was determined to kill Mary
Stuart, if ever she gave him the chance. She did.
In 1586 there arose, latest and last of all the
Marian confederacies, the Babington plot. There
had been once in Mary's service a page of the
name of Anthony Babington ; he was now a
recusant gentleman of Derbyshire. He took up
the captive sovereign's cause ; others joined him.
The Spanish ambassador wished the assassination
of the Queen to be extended to Cecil, Walsingham,
and a few others. Philip was inclined to spare
Cecil – "he is very old" – but otherwise he hoped
for the best. "Perhaps," he wrote hopefully,

with an allusion to God, " the time has at last come when He will strike for His cause." Walsingham, on his side, thought exactly the same ; he also watched, and probably encouraged, the schemes. Hopes were equally high on both sides ; and the death of a Queen was a necessary element in both.

In a cask of beer the letters went to and from Mary ; at the right moment the Secretary struck. The conspirators were seized. Fourteen were executed ; the first seven with the full accompaniments of horror, the second seven on the next day being, by Elizabeth's personal command, allowed to hang till they were dead before the ritual of agony was carried out.

Mary remained. Elizabeth consented to her trial. While the Commission was sitting at Fotheringay, she sent a sudden message recalling its members to London. The Queen was confronted with the worst crisis of her life. It is as certain as any mortal thing can be, not merely that she did not want to execute Mary, but that she thought she ought not to execute Mary. She was physically revolted by the idea, and more or less consciously she knew it was a contradiction of her life's basis. Mary was anointed and royal ; she was not Elizabeth's subject, she was Elizabeth's equal, and as sacrosanct as the Queen herself. In her blood and fibres Elizabeth felt it to be a sin to touch this other Majesty – a dreadful, perhaps a mortal, sin. She was normally as casual of morals as of dogmas, but her scepticism had its limits, and all she had ever persuaded others, or herself believed, that she herself was, rose against the deed.

Her Ministers, her Council, her Parliament, her bishops, her people – the preachers and the crowds – were united in pressing the deed on her. The two elements of her desire clashed. She was Queen ; she was Queen of England. The people of England were contradicting the principle of kingship. At Richmond the Parliament poured its petition before her. She answered that it was a miracle that she was still alive.[1] She added that she took no such pleasure in life that she much desired it, nor conceived such horror in death that she greatly feared it ; " Yet I say not, but if the stroke were coming, perchance flesh and blood would be moved with it, and seek to shun it. I have had good experience and trial of this world." It is one of her most universal moments.

From October to February she demurred and disputed with herself. She listened to the protests of ambassadors and snarled at the messengers

[1] It was a common feeling. In 1584 William of Orange had been assassinated. In 1586 the French ambassador at Rome wrote to the King of France concerning Elizabeth : "She cannot doubt that at every moment some attempt will be made on her life, and that she cannot again enjoy an hour of safety or of pleasure." The Pope himself said he had abhorrently rejected proposals for her assassination, which had been, on occasions, made to him.

HE

of the Scottish King. At the very end she fell
back on the possibility of private murder, and
caused Walsingham to write to Paulet, Mary's
jailer, suggesting that it might be within the
bounds of his duty to take off his prisoner. It
was not the justice of the sentence against Mary
that troubled her, as certainly it troubled hardly
anyone else. That Mary was guilty of com-
plicity everyone knew. But that an anointed
sovereign should put to death, by show of trial,
another anointed sovereign – this was the crisis.
In the position to which Elizabeth had come
there were, for her, but two possibilities – a
supreme determination after virtue or certain sin.
She sinned. She signed the warrant. Walsingham was away ; he was ill. She cried to his
substitute to show him the warrant. " The grief
thereof will go near to kill him outright."

The opinion of royal Europe supported her
own ; Mary should have been put to death
privately. Elizabeth was not only heretical but
barbarous ; not only false to doctrine but false
to her royal blood – a bastard of kingship. She
was blamed for the manner, not for the fact, of
the death. And, indeed, in that act, as in so
many others, she had abandoned doctrine ; this
time against, as often with, her will. She had
been the friend of events, and now events had
betrayed her into offending against her own
strong belief. There was to be but one other

personal crisis in her life when another axe was
to swing, and in that no doctrine was to have any
place, and events were to run altogether wild.
The daughter of things, she was to be finally hurt
by things.

At the same time even bastards have their
place. The King of France was not disposed to
be unfriendly with the Queen while the King of
Spain still threatened. But with the King of
Spain the time for friendship had gone by. At
last he was moved to refuse to be a brother to
Elizabeth any more. It was known he was
making preparations, and now the death of Mary
left him as the great Roman Catholic claimant –
by descent perhaps, but anyhow by providential
conquest. The King of France and the Pope
contemplated the prospect with some gloom, but
the Pope at least was compelled to lend his support – money and briefs. The " Enterprise of
England " took shape. Drake raided Cadiz, and
delayed it ; the chosen Admiral died, and delayed
it further ; storms delayed it still more. But
gradually it began to move. The slow navies of
the metaphysical world gathered in the harbours
of Spain ; the Duke of Medina Sidonia took
command. The armies of metaphysics stood
ready in Flanders ; the Prince of Parma controlled them with military care. The last of the
Crusades was about to begin. All the material
resources of the champions of metaphysics were

employed – the Pope had promised a million gold
ducats, Philip had taxed the food of his subjects :
all their intellectual resources – the Pope freed all
Catholics from their temporary allegiance ;
Cardinal Allen yet once more described and
denounced the Queen in a printed *Admonition to
the People of England* – " an incestuous bastard,
begotten and born in sin of an infamous courtesan " ; all spiritual aid was invoked – by processions, prayers, vigils, adorations. The double
figure of sin had sat too long on the waters –
thrice opprobrious : in her blood, in her belief,
in her wickedness. Illegitimate, heretical, bloody,
and debauched, she sat there like some horrible
Scylla devouring the martyrs, and around her
flew the ships of her vile company, Drake, Hawkins, Grenville. One voice only broke the
chorus ; in the centre of the Crusade, of all
people, the Pope Sixtus V himself exclaimed in
admiration, both of her and of Drake : " What
a woman ! " " Have you heard how Drake has
offered battle ? What courage ! " " If she were
not a heretic she would be worth the whole
world ! " The Queen is said to have courteously
reciprocated, saying she knew but of one man
worthy of her – and he was Sixtus V.

In spite of the Papal admiration, the Spanish
Navy swept out. The King kept vigil before
the Blessed Sacrament, and the mighty array
passed north. No other metaphysic met them,

for, though Cecil and Walsingham had done
what they could, it was the ships of Howard
and Hawkins and Drake that ran beside them,
firing and wounding, and the unmetaphysical
winds that drove them. They fled ; they dis-
appeared. " God blew with His winds and they
were scattered," said the medal struck by Elizabeth. It seems unlikely that privately the Queen
more than half believed it. Once, in a later year,
one of her present captains, Sir John Hawkins,
coming back from a voyage with less gain than had
been hoped, sent an explanation of his failure
in some such terms : " Paul might plant and
Apollos might water, but only God gives the
increase." To which the Queen said only :
" Fool ! He went out a soldier and comes home
a divine." Less than most people by now did she
think the universe likely to observe her desires.
Her life's disillusion forbade it, yet perhaps her
disillusion hardly went far enough. It did not
lead her to the rock which is reality. For Elizabeth, while she lived, that path was too strange,
rather than too hard, a way. Events now had
gone favourably ; they might as well have gone
unfavourably. Bitter and amused, fearful and
courageous, she looked at them. They had involved her in much evil fate and in something
like dishonour. She was Elizabeth ; she raged
and endured.

In that heart-sickness of necessity she was still –

it was her duty and her pleasure – a spectacle.
In that certainly she was of her age. She determined to go to her Army and went. She was
fifty-five, and old for that. She was bald, bony,
rheumatic. But she was strongly active, and
her centre of vitality was very firm. She came
down to them ; it was the ninth of August, and the
Armada was already driven far away up the North
Seas, but there was Parma yet in the Netherlands,
and it was uncertain what he could or would do.
She rode down, and, mounted on a white horse,
reviewed the Army. There she delivered that
famous speech, with its high Elizabethan combination of rhetoric and realism ; she threw off her
sin and made herself a hero. It was all wrong and
yet all right at once, as the Queen so often was.
She sat on her horse, and (so they report) she
said : " My loving people, we have been persuaded by some that are careful of our safety,
to take heed how we commit ourselves to armed
multitudes, for fear of treachery. But I assure
you, I do not desire to live to distrust my faithful
and loving people. Let tyrants fear. I have
always so behaved myself that, under God, I have
placed my chiefest strength and safeguard in the
loyal hearts and goodwill of my subjects ; and
therefore I am come amongst you, as you see, at
this time, not for my recreation and disport, but
being resolved, in the midst and heat of the
battle, to live or die amongst you all, to lay down

for my God, and for my kingdom, and for my people, my honour and my blood, even in the dust. I know I have the body of a weak and feeble woman, but I have the heart and stomach of a king, and of a king of England too, and think foul scorn that Parma or Spain, or any prince of Europe should dare to invade the borders of my realm ; to which, rather than any dishonour shall grow by me, I myself will take up arms, I myself will be your general, judge, and rewarder of every one of your virtues in the field. I know, already for your forwardness you have deserved rewards and crowns ; and we do assure you, in the word of a prince, they shall be duly paid you."

On the fourth of September, in the same year, Leicester died.

CHAPTER VII

THE defeat of the Armada and the death of
Leicester seem to close the period of the Queen's
purpose ; the letter upon which she wrote " His
last letter " is still extant.   What remained was a
period of result – fourteen years and more, nearly
a third of her whole reign.   Throughout that
third, however, her position did not much change.
The defeat of the Armada opened a war with
Spain which dragged on through the years.
Had Philip been free to concentrate his attention
and his power upon England, the final decision
might yet have gone the other way.   He was not ;
the affairs of Spanish diplomacy involved two
worlds – or indeed three, the Old and the New,
and the next.   In France, assassination had its
way ; Henry III had the Duke of Guise and the
Cardinal of Guise killed, and was himself stabbed
in 1589, by a Dominican, as an enemy of the Pope.
The fortunes of the kingdom went down and then
rose ; Philip laboured against the succession of
Henry of Navarre, and failed.   Henry submitted
to Rome – " Paris vaut bien une messe " –

and became Henry IV ; his conversion shook the old doctrinal order as much as his earlier Protestantism.   The English sent a military expedition against Spain in 1589, which returned with heavy damage but high prestige.   The mere landing in Spain and the defeat of a Spanish army were great things.   In 1590 ten English merchantmen defeated twelve Spanish galleys in the Strait of Gibraltar.   In 1596 came the expedition against, and the capture of, Cadiz. The war party in England was no longer desperate, religious, and middle-aged ; it was young, secular, and brilliant with victory and victorious hopes.   Expectation sat in the air.

Another struggle which had maintained itself through the reign – less spectacular and less bloody, but hardly less bitter than that with Spain and Rome – also ceased gradually to trouble the Queen – that with the Puritan champions.   This, indeed, was not to reach a climax of separating definition till the time or King James, though in the very days of the Armada the most notorious demonstrations broke out in the Martin Marprelate pamphlets.   The " Canterbury Caiaphas," the " froth and filth " of ecclesiastical laws, " the squealing of chanting choristers," the " idle loitering lubbards " of cathedrals, the " cursed uncircumcised murdering generation " of the clergy, " the horned monsters of the Conspiration House," " the pageant and stage-play " of the Communion, were all " run down with a saucy pertness." No extreme of danger could reconcile the Queen to those wilder extremes of Protestant doctrine. Not even Cecil's influence could win her to sympathy. It was impossible for her to believe that " to ring more bells than one on the Lord's day was as great a sin as murder." Metaphysically, it might be ; practically, the Queen felt it was not. By suppression and banishment, by discussion and exposition, this quarrel also was silenced. Numbers of Puritans fled abroad ; numbers were mournfully still. Hooker and Andrewes began to be heard.

Beyond the European seas, the English name flew farther and farther. Virginia had been first founded in 1585 by Walter Raleigh. In the Old World the trade with Russia had been maintained all through the reign ; in 1582 a permanent ambassador was established at Constantinople, in spite of French and Venetian opposition ; in 1580 it had been suggested to captains in the Muscovy trade that " opportunity may be had to sail over to Japan " – where the Jesuits had preceded them. Jesuit missionaries and English merchants rivalled each other in energy abroad, as at home, Jesuit ardour contended with national ardour ; nor were the nationals and the merchants always without religious devotion, sometimes false, sometimes

true, sometimes narrow and harsh, sometimes
intelligent and lovely.   The City of London laid
hold on Java : the sentences of Hakluyt recount
the tale of the distances : " . . . to speake a word
of that just commendation which our nation doe
indeed deserve : it can not be denied, but as in
all former ages, they have bene men full of
activity, stirrers abroad, and searchers of the
remote parts of the world, so in this most famous
and peerlesse governement of her most excellent
Majesty, her subjects through the speciall assistance, and blessing of God, in searching the most
opposite corners and quarters of the world, and
to speake plainly, in compassing the vaste globe
of the earth more then once, have excelled all
the nations and people of the earth.   For, which
of the kings of this land before her Majesty, had
theyr banners ever seene in the Caspian sea ?
which of them hath ever dealt with the Emperor
of Persia, as her Majesty hath done, and obteined
for her merchants large and loving privileges ?
who ever found English Consuls and Agents at
Tripolis in Syria, at Aleppo, at Babylon, at
Balsara, and which is more, who ever heard of
Englishman at Goa before now ? what English
shippes did heeretofore ever anker in the mighty
river of Plate ? passe and repasse the unpassable
(in former opinion) straight of Magellan, range
along the coast of Chili, Peru, and all the back-
side of Nova Hispania, further then any Christian

ever passed, travers the mighty bredth of the South sea, land upon the Luzones in despight of the enemy, enter into alliance, amity, and traffike with the princes of the Moluccaes, and the Isle of Java, double the famous Cape of Bona Speranza, arive at the Isle of Santa Helena, and last of al returne home most richly laden with the commodities of China, as the subjects of this now flourishing monarchy have done ? "

At home, other conquests were being made. While the City trafficked with Java, the genius of the poets trafficked with experience. In 1590 *Tamburlaine* was presented " on stages in the city " ; in 1590 the first cantos of the *Faerie Queene* adored the Queen of faerie and of England ; in 1594 appeared before the Court at Greenwich " William Kemp, William Shakespeare, and Richarde Burbage, servants to the Lord Chamberleyne." The years became full of presentation and publication, and the name of the old Queen became a synonym for one of the few supreme imaginative explorations of man. She was dead before the full achievement of it, but it is still, and justly, her name that presides. James Stuart had his own virtues, but they were not of her scope, nor was the royalty of his presence phenomenal like hers. " The imperial votaress passed on " – aged, jewel-encrusted, perverse, egotistic, Gloriana. It was no smooth, placid simplicity they praised under that name, but rather a twisted, dangerous splendour, almost a monstrosity – violent, tender, intelligent, rapacious. The late Renascence blazed about her, interwoven with the deaths which accompanied it and waited for it. She went in their midst, and they sang : she was Gloriana.

She had always been lonely, but now her loneliness grew. Shakespeare acted before her ; Francis Bacon was among her lawyers. But they were not her intimates. Leicester was dead ; Walsingham was dead ; her favourite Hatton was dead ; her enemy and kinswoman Mary was dead ; her enemy and ally Catherine de Medici was dead. Cecil was very old ; he had brought his second son Robert into his business, as it were, and almost into office. The Queen named him " my beagle," one of that menagerie of small strange beasts it had been an amusement of her vivid mind to title. Alençon had been her frog ; and Alençon's servant, Simier, her monkey ; and James VI's servant, the Master of Gray, her hare. And there were other names : Hatton was her sheep ; Walsingham her Moor ; the elder Cecil had been her spirit ; and the lost Leicester her eyes. So now the beagle came into the business, and set himself to the management, and to the management of the whims and the intellect of the chief shareholder. The work was not made easier by the existence of an opposite party. " There was a party " – in all senses of the word. There were intimate parties given in the Queen's rooms ; there was a political party at the Council-board ; and there was a " party " – the old vulgarity has a sense of the contempt and the hostility – whose name was Essex.

He had come through Leicester ; he was Leicester's legacy, and might have been Leicester's rival, had Leicester lived, for he was Leicester's stepson. It was said that his stepfather had poisoned his father. He had been married to Walsingham's daughter, the widow of Philip Sidney, who survived him. He was twenty-one in the year of the Armada, and in the years after the Armada he became the first – and the last – of the Queen's minions.

In 1593, the Queen was sixty. She did not easily abandon her habits, and some of them had by now hardened into tyrannies and even obsessions. The question of the succession had always angered her ; now she would not allow it to be raised. It had meant talk and thought of Mary of Scots, and illegitimacy, and possible death, and now she would have no more of it. There was no longer any close claimant to the Throne. Legitimate or illegitimate, she and the chance of things had imposed her claim upon things. She was Queen of England ; at least, there was no one else. She indulged herself, and forbade any talk of anyone else, to the serious inconvenience of her Ministers and the serious irritation of James of Scotland. But while she indulged herself in discouraging talk of death, she indulged herself also in encouraging talk of love. Her culture had delighted in flattery, and now the demand for flattery became an obsession. Abuse of culture, abuse of intimacy, tended to grow in her ; yet she never lost intelligence. By such a mistress, greedy of adoration, greedy of service, greedy of intelligence, the handsome young soldier Essex was distinguished. He accepted favour.

Had he had to do with some kinds of women, Essex might have risen into godhead and retained it to the end. As he rose, his opinion of Elizabeth fell. He mistook her ancient, uncomely amorousness, not only for weakness, which it was, but for thorough weakness, which it was not. When he quarrelled with her, which he did often, and violently, as none before him had dared, he flung away and left her, and waited to be summoned back, though he could be pretty enough in his worship when he came. He set up a foreign secret service of his own, shaped and conducted by the skill of Anthony Bacon, elder brother of Francis. Together Essex and Anthony played against Cecil, Essex at the Council, Anthony in Essex House, conducting correspondence with half Europe. It was believed that Essex managed the Queen and that Anthony managed Essex, and it was to Anthony that great lords and ladies

made application for favours desired. For a little
it looked as if Anthony Bacon might defeat Robert
Cecil and rule England through Essex and the
Queen. Francis Bacon was not much use to
anyone, and even Essex showed him magnificent
gratitude rather because of his brother than of
himself. But it was Francis who saw the danger
to which things were coming. " My lord," he
wrote afterwards, " had a settled opinion that the
Queen could be brought to nothing but by a kind
of necessity and authority."

Necessity she had known, but never authority ;
she had never had any personal relation which
imposed it on her, and there she had never even
been false to it. It was her greater loneliness,
and Essex could not bring any such authority
to bear ; how should he, who knew nothing of it
himself ? In September 1597, the older Cecil
died. Essex was then sulking, after a scene in the
Council chamber during which the Queen had
struck him and he had caught at his sword.
More alone than ever before, she permitted
herself to be reconciled, and let him go as he
wished to Ireland. He went ; he failed ; he
returned. For a moment she yielded and welcomed him fondly ; then she remembered herself,
and put him in custody. She was the Queen.

Events had run wild ; there was neither
political nor religious cause of dissension. Elizabeth had, all her life, appealed to untheoretical

life ; from untheoretical life she received her reward. She had let the axe fall on Mary for the sake of her own person and rule ; for the same cause she had to let the axe fall on Essex. The tragedy lingered for two years through its slow stages : custody, examination, freedom with banishment from Court, rumours, gatherings. Essex House became full of discontented men. Essex – a mad comment upon the helplessness of events – appealed both to Puritans and Catholics. No more utter destruction of metaphysics could appear. He wrote an appealing, adoring letter to the Queen, and tacked on to it – to such a woman ! – a request for a renewal of his monopoly of sweet wines. Robert Cecil – more Cecilian and less theological than his great father – struck with more intelligence and with even more effect than his father had done of old.

In 1601 Essex, threatened again by the Council and kept separate from the Queen, rode out of his house into the City, found no help there, and eventually surrendered. By craft or by accident a minor plot by an odd soldier against the Queen's life was discovered immediately after. Essex was tried and condemned ; this time there was no delay. If Elizabeth woke by night, she sent no message ; if she hesitated, she proposed no private destruction. She signed the warrant ; three weeks after the outbreak, Essex, having first blamed everybody else, died.

IE

The Council caused a statement of the Earl's treasonable practices to be drawn up. The writer – it was Francis Bacon, who had played a perfectly consistent and loyal part throughout the drama, and been universally blamed as a result – used in phrases the style " my lord of Essex." She struck at her false lover once more : " Write Essex." It was so done.

CHAPTER VIII

After Essex – peace and war – taxation and monopolies – the
last speech to the Commons – " these fooleries " – Cecil
determines the succession – death of the Queen.

SHE was sixty-seven. The emotional crisis, or
the loss of Essex, or the last necessary effort to
maintain the quiet of the State, had all but
exhausted her. She was still active in mind and
body. In the December following the revolt she
was at the Blackfriars Theatre, after having dined
with the Lord Chamberlain. It is not known
what play the company, in which now the greatest
of her subjects held an important place, gave her.
Shakespeare was only reaching the time of the
tragedies. She had passed her own. She had –
could she have known it ? – given her own life
to the cause to which she had given so much :
the strange cause which was herself or her people
or a kind of uncertain dream of freedom, or all
compact, so that neither she nor they nor we can
tell where sincerity ended and insincerity began.
Like the line between belief and disbelief which
had evaded the certain knowledge of her scruti-
neers in her young years, this other line has
evaded all eyes ever since. The death of Essex
lay on the sincere side ; she suffered. Her pain

grew into her. She remained, throughout it, in possession of her position and her people.

Yet her people, the very mass that her reign had deflected into a nation, with national prestige and national greed, were a little restless behind her. It was thirteen or fourteen years since the Armada, forty-four or forty-five since her accession. Generations that had not known the old fears or the old quarrels had arisen. On the religious side many desired honourable peace : " What have wars, invasions, books, done these twenty years ? You have heard ; we to our sorrow have seen and endured," wrote one priest to Rome. The Queen was merciful ; what might not the Pope do, if only the Jesuits could be bridled ! The Jesuits gained no more ground ; they merely held their own. The Roman idea was becoming, as for long it unfortunately remained, the myth of a minority. Nothing was ever yet gained by misunderstanding a creed, nor does the Catholicity of the Church of England need to be maintained by ignorance. Rome must be decently known to be decently refused. The everlasting question of the succession caused dissension even here, and the Jesuit mission which supported a Spanish succession was opposed by the secular clergy, who leaned towards James of Scotland. Occasionally the quarrels between the two parties even resulted in appeals by the seculars to the Queen herself. One of them had an audience, in which, speaking of the Pope, she exclaimed justly, " Your chief pastor pronounced sentence against me while I was yet in my mother's womb."

The rest of the nation vibrated sometimes uneasily behind the antique figure. The death of Essex, least tolerable to Elizabeth of all the three grand executions, Norfolk's and Mary's and his, yet the most morally justified, was, ironically, the least popular. The Queen's justice was defeated by the weapons she herself had used in her youth – spectacle and an appeal to the vulgar. Essex had been showy and handsome and liberal and brave ; he had been for political war, and always for more war. The new stout-hearted generations backed him ; it was their fathers whom the craft of the subtle young Queen had wisely kept out of war, and their fathers were dying. " Point de guerre," Elizabeth had on occasion cried to her Council of old, but that was slow policy now. Essex was a hero, a dead Essex more certainly a hero than a living. In 1601, when the Queen went to open Parliament, there was silence in the streets.

A more prolonged quarrel was opening : the financial. War was wanted, but not taxation. The Queen all through her reign had kept herself as free as possible from dependence on subsidies ; it was part of her superiority and her popularity. She asked for subsidies now. They were voted, but an attack was made on her methods, or on one of her methods – that of monopolies. Monopolies exist to-day, and money has been made out of them to-day, only all that is more hidden. The Elizabethan age was less ashamed of money than ours ; it clamoured for it frankly and fought for it openly. The Queen had granted monopolies – for rewards, for revenue, for protection of manufactures – but they were unpopular. The time had come when they could be attacked, and they were. In the Parliament of 1601 there was a great noise ; the Government were abused. Robert Cecil was never a good man at managing the House ; the attack dangerously approached the Prerogative. All her life Elizabeth had managed to " put herself over " ; she had baffled inquirers, perplexed ambassadors, maddened her Ministers, and thrilled her people. The public Elizabeth, the Queen who was Elizabeth rather than the Elizabeth who was Queen, rose again. On 24 November, 1601, the House had been in high confusion, and was gathering its courage to defy the Government, however Cecil might warn them of the danger of such a course. On 25 November he rose with a message from the Throne : the Queen consented to remedy their grievances. She consented – as a grace : she acted by proclamation – and kept the Prerogative intact. Five days later the Commons, on their knees in Whitehall, beheld for the last time above them the adorned figure of their high and mighty Princess, and heard her speaking to them :

" Mr. Speaker, We perceive your coming is to present thanks to us. Know I accept them with no less joy than your loves can have desire to offer such a present, and do more esteem it than any treasure or riches ; for those we know how to prize, but loyalty, love, and thanks, I account them invaluable. And though God hath raised me high, yet this I account the glory of my crown, that I have reigned with your loves. This makes me that I do not so much rejoice that God hath made me to be a Queen, as to be a Queen over so thankful a people, and to be the means under God to conserve you in safety and to preserve you from danger. . . . I never was any greedy, scraping grasper, nor a strict, fast-holding prince, nor yet a waster ; my heart was never set upon any worldly goods, but only for my subjects' good."

With such a superb presentation of herself, her public life drew to a close. The Commons dispersed in gratitude and adoration ; never before had she more greatly succeeded with an audience, and, if the actual truth was something lower than the graph of her rhetoric showed, it ran at least in a parallel curve. She believed utterly in herself as that kind of Queen, and her belief was not only sincere but largely justified.

Few sovereigns have loved the common people better than Elizabeth ; few have been more full of princely goodwill than she was to her servants. It is true they had to be utterly *her* servants.

It was 30 November, 1601 ; by a twelvemonth later her constitution was breaking down. Through the year she still danced, rode, hunted, wrote letters in her own hand – " I end, scribbling in haste. Your loving sovereign " – gave audiences, thought of going on progresses. The cheers rose round her again. By the end of 1602, when she was drawing towards seventy, she began to know that things were at an end. Her godson, Sir John Harrington, read her his verses ; she listened with a smile and said : " When thou dost feel creeping time at thy gate, these fooleries will please thee less. I am past my relish for such matters." By the end of February 1603 it was remarked that she no longer took interest in serious political discussion ; she " delighteth to hear old Canterbury tales." Robert Carey came to see her. She was sitting on her cushions on the floor – it was an old habit of hers ; she took his hand, saying, " No, Robin, I am not well," and sighed continually in a heaviness of heart. Between the eleventh and twenty-third of March she grew worse. She lay silent, refusing medicine, refusing food, exclaiming sometimes when they pressed her. There are a score of tales, of uncertain value, of the closing days.

The Council came to her, and for the last time the word " succession " struck her dimming ears. It was the word that had been with her since she could first begin to understand the world ; in the days of Harry her father, of Mary Tudor her sister, of Mary Stuart her cousin. One way or another it had dominated her life ; it had kept her unmarried and set the danger of death round her. No one lived more in the immediate present than Elizabeth, but that present had had always with it the spectral future, as a promise, as a right, as a danger, as a thing hated. Cecil and the Council had determined what they would do ; they had determined for two years past to introduce that learned metaphysician – and he was – James of Scotland. They asked her if she consented. It is said she made an ambiguous movement, raising her hands to her head. It is said she did so in sign of assent ; either that, or at the very last moment, did she still mazedly seek to protect her own Crown ? The Council went ; the Archbishop came. She kept him there, praying ; at last even that dim awareness passed, and she lay unconscious. Two hours after midnight, at the nadir of the twenty-four hours, on Thursday, 24 March, she entered into death.

CHAPTER IX

Epilogue – the intentions of the Queen and their conclusions –
Java and the Lateran – " so sweet a bait."

SHE had had no formal intention of multiplying
dominion or maintaining doctrine ; she had, in
effect, done both – had promulgated an empire
and preserved a Church. She had lent ships to
bring gold and they had sown government. She
had had personal preferences in religion, and they
had so mingled with the affairs of the time as to
prevent both the Papal and the extreme Protestant
influences. No more than the revolution of
Geneva was the resolution of the Council of
Trent allowed to define in England the less settled
medieval pattern. She had drawn India and
Java into English trade, and excluded from
English religion the Lateran on the Cœlian hill.
All this she did without intention, and because,
though she loved herself in the common egoistic
way of men, she loved herself also as an objective
fact. She loved herself as a person, but also as
a Queen. And though there again her love was
half selfish, though often when she looked in the
glass it was Elizabeth crowned she saw, it was
often the crowned Queen of England. That,
because she liked the English, she loved, and the

popular cheers of the English told her that they loved it too. She wrote once to Burghley in one of his fits of gloom : " Serve God, feare the Kinge, and be a Good fellow to the rest " ; it was her ideal of a man. Even among the recusants her popularity was not dead, and, unless she were maddened by fear or anger, she had motions of mercy there ; it is said she once saved seventy priests and sent them over to the Continent. This again may have been calculated generosity ; their living voice might sound louder in Papal Europe than the spiritual accusations of the dead. Her calculations went very far, yet she was a woman of the sixteenth century, and in the last analysis even her calculations were rather intuitive than intellectual, however the intellect subserved its twin. Most women tend to be Calvinistic in their outlook upon this world, however this heresy may be checked by their intelligence, and even Elizabeth's sceptical nature beheld the world as composed of the elect, who were her friends, and the reprobate, who were her enemies. If these last were in power or with desirable influence, she could pretend to be ready to be friends ; once only, in the incident of Alençon, did she pretend to be friends. In the phrase of John Harington, quoting Hatton, " The Queen did fish for men's souls, and had so sweet a bait that no one could escape her network." They swam to that net ;

even if she cast them back into the waters, they
came shooting towards her again, avid of capture. She enjoyed culture and jollity ; she found
physical or mental abandonment difficult ; in
that self-grasp, she could be cruel. She was
lonely, for she was royal, and neither pious nor
impious. One would like to know if ever she
held philosophical talk with Maitland of Lethington, or if ever anything but formal talk, if that,
passed between her and Shakespeare. Without
his genius of exploration and expression, she had
in her life a kind of kinship with the method of
his genius. She is an active and debased carica-
ture of the purity of his power, as egoistic as that
was necessarily unegoistic. It is not absurd that,
over an abyss, he should praise her. In a midsummer night's dream he saw her ; her own
midsummer's day was more fevered and more
tortuous. Yet the general title of the plays, and
of their method, might be *The Way Things Happen.*
It is hers also. She happened, and she continued
to happen. It was the sense of the unlikely
chance of her that lingered, whether (as Cardinal
Allen wrote) as an incestuous bastard begotten
of an infamous courtesan or (as the French ambassador said) receiving " blessings from the
people as though she had been another Messiah."
Then and since, it has distinguished her. She
was, then and since, unexpected, in her birth,
in her succession, in her boast of singleness, in

her bravery of success. Unassassinated and undeposed, untheological in an age of theologies, uncertain in a world of certainties, turning upon some hidden centre of her own, faithful to some dark belief of her own, and else as incalculable in her actions as unforeseen in her existence ; brilliant and disingenuous, humble and sincere, a perverse portent, she sat on the English Throne for forty years, and moved the English imagination for four centuries, an incarnate, memorable, and terrifying example of the way things happen. As common and as unusual as that, she was Elizabeth.

www.ingramcontent.com/pod-product-compliance
Lightning Source LLC
Chambersburg PA
CBHW032103080426
42733CB00006B/400